WHAT IS
"THE CHURCH"?

WHAT IS
"THE CHURCH"?

EDDIE CLOER

RESOURCE ☐
PUBLICATIONS
2205 S. Benton
Searcy, AR 72143

Dedication

To My Wife
Susan
My heart's inspiration,
A Christian mother unexcelled,
A co-laborer with extraordinary abilities
and genuine Christlikeness,
A Christian woman
who models Christianity
in the home,
at work,
and at play.

DOXOLOGY:
"Blessed be the God and Father
of our Lord Jesus Christ, who has blessed us
with every spiritual blessing in the heavenly places
in Christ, . . ." (Ephesians 1:3).

Contents

Preface

Three themes predominate in the Scriptures: the coming of Christ, the coming of the kingdom of God or the church, and the salvation of the world. These three themes are so interrelated and so intertwined in the Bible that any attempt to gain a thorough understanding of one necessitates gaining an understanding of all three, and a grasp of one implies a fairly good understanding of the other two. They present what God has done, what He is doing, and what He intends to do in the world. Together they reflect the heart of the Bible.

The Scriptures present the church and the kingdom of God as basically the same entity, although the two terms view the entity from two different vantage points. "The kingdom of God" is a broader concept than "the church," emphasizing the rule of God or Christ in heaven and on earth; while "the church" suggests the chosen people of God, the grouped followers of Christ. We might say that the church is the earthly form of the kingdom of God. The terms "church" and "kingdom of heaven" are interchanged by our Lord in Matthew 16:17-19. His usage reveals that one can interchange the terms without a corruption of the use of either:

And Jesus answered and said to him, "Blessed are you, Simon Barjona, because flesh and blood did not reveal this to you, but My Father who is in heaven. And I also say to you that you are Peter, and upon this rock I will build My church; and the gates of Hades shall not overpower it. I will give you the keys of the kingdom of heaven; and whatever you shall bind on earth shall be bound in heaven, and whatever you shall loose on earth shall be loosed in heaven."

The church is the fulfillment of the life and work of Jesus. It is the fruit of His mission in this world. Thus, a detailed understanding of the church is crucial to faithful service to Christ.

This study of the church will be limited to a consideration of the definitions and the basic nature of the church as the kingdom of God. It is Book One in a series on the unique nature and divine design of the church. Other studies are also planned, the Lord willing (James 4:15), on related subjects, such as the worship of the church, its organization, and its mission in the world.

I have no other intention in this world than to be a Christian, the kind the New Testament teaches us to be. I am seeking to be a part of the New Testament church of Christ without any denominational affiliation. My commitment is to wear His name and to give glory only to Christ, my Savior.

This book is a human production, and consequently, will have weaknesses and failings; but it is hoped that the reader will overlook these and see the author's intentions. It was written with the prayer that our Father may use it, in spite of its faults, to call all who read it who are away from Him into the church which the Bible presents and to lead those who are in Christ's church to a deeper appreciation of where they are.

In any special undertaking, one is the beneficiary of the kind assistance of others. The writing of this book has been no exception. Exceptional assistance in proofing, suggestions for the final form, and in finalizing numerous other little details that converting a manuscript into a permanent book entails were provided by my wife, Susan, and Cheryl Schramm, our efficient typographer and co-laborer in the Lord. My sincere gratitude is expressed to them.

Merciful Father in heaven,

Receive, we pray, our gratitude for Your abundant grace and wonderful salvation. You have sent Christ into the world to purchase with His blood a people for His name and for His work, a people zealous for truth and good works.

Thank You for Your perfect revelation, the Holy Scriptures which unfold Your design for Christ's church. Give us honest hearts with which to seek Your guidance and eternal purpose. Teach us to lay aside all types of prejudice, all secret agendas and personal bias, that we may accept Your will regarding Your purposes and plans.

We aspire to serve You and You alone. Lead us in the paths of Your revealed truth. Make us unmistakably the church of Christ.

Through Christ's name we pray, Amen.

"To God and our Savior Jesus Christ be the glory."

Eddie Cloer

1

What Is "The Church"?

"And He put all things in subjection under His feet, and gave Him as head over all things to the church, which is His body, the fulness of Him who fills all in all" (Ephesians 1:22, 23).

A man from another country and culture wanted to come to the USA for an extended visit. Having worked hard to learn English, he believed that he was ready for his trip. He made his long-awaited trip to America, and soon after his arrival, his knowledge of English was put to the test. He went into a small grocery store to buy several items. At the check-out counter, he was told how much he owed. Efficiently, he reached into his pocket, took out his money, counted the right amount, and handed it to the clerk. He put his groceries in a sack and started to leave. As he was going out the door, the clerk kindly said, "Come back!" The visitor stopped, turned around, and came back to the counter. The clerk said, "May I help you?" Somewhat confused, the man said, "You told me to come back!"

The man had taken an expression which meant "Thank you for your business; let us help you again soon," and had interpreted it literally. His mistake in understanding the clerk's intended meaning resulted in a failure in communication.

All of us have had his kind of experience. We knew the words which were spoken to us, but we did not understand how those words were being used by the one speaking to us. We understood the words but completely missed the meaning that was being conveyed.

Any way you look at it, communication is difficult. Much is required of the speaker and of the hearer for actual communication to take place.

Honesty with God demands that we carefully search for the meaning which God intended for His message.

Let us apply the process of communication to the study of the Bible. For profitable communication between the Bible and us to take place, we must not only listen to the words that were used, but we must also seek the meaning which the inspired writer had in mind as he chose these words. This means that we must make an effort to understand the context in which a word or sentence appears. Honesty with God demands that we carefully search for the meaning which God intended for His message.

The word "church" is familiar to most of us. God talks to us at length about this word in the Scriptures. For communication to occur between God and us regarding this word, we must be willing to go into the biblical world and see the word meanings, illustrations, and thought forms which were used by Jesus, the apostles, and the other inspired men who wrote the Bible through God's Spirit.

What is "the church"? As the New Testament uses this word 114 times[1] in various contexts, in seventeen of its twenty-seven books,[2] what is being communicated to us? When Jesus established the church, what did He build?

A SPIRITUAL BODY

First, we must recognize that the church is a spiritual body, the very spiritual body of Christ.

A picture which usually comes to our minds with the word "church" is a physical building in which worship takes place. The word is never used in the New Testament, though, to convey this meaning.

In the Scriptures, the word "church" denotes the body of those who have yielded to the gospel of Christ and have been redeemed by the blood of Christ in their assembled, local, and universal senses.

First, the body of the redeemed as they assemble or gather to worship God is called "the church." As Paul rebuked the church at Corinth for their lack of unity when they gathered, he used the word "church" for the assembly of Christians. He said, ". . . when you come together as a church, I hear that divisions exist among you; . . ." (1 Corinthians 11:18).

---

[1]Ethelbert W. Bullinger, *A Critical Lexicon and Concordance to the English and Greek New Testament* (Grand Rapids, Mich.: Zondervan, 1975), 153.

[2]Ibid. Mark, Luke, John, 2 Timothy, Titus, 1 and 2 Peter, 1 and 2 John, and Jude do not have the word "church" in them.

Second, "church" is used for the body of the redeemed in a definite locale. The body of redeemed ones at Corinth is called "the church of God which is at Corinth" (1 Corinthians 1:2). Still further, "church" is used for the totality of the redeemed ones throughout the world. Paul referred to the church in a universal sense when he said, "For the husband is the head of the wife, as Christ also is the head of the church, He Himself being the Savior of the body" (Ephesians 5:23).

Let us apply these New Testament uses of the word "church" to a specific event in Acts. The many residents and visitors in Jerusalem on the Day of Pentecost (Acts 2:1-4) heard the external manifestations of the outpouring of the Holy Spirit and gathered around the apostles to see what was taking place. As Peter preached to the multitude, he convinced them that Jesus was both Lord and Christ (Acts 2:36). In anguish of soul, many cried out, "What shall we do?" (Acts 2:37). Since faith prompted their crying out, Peter did not need to tell them to believe, but he did need to tell them to do what they had not done— to repent and be baptized for the forgiveness of their sins (Acts 2:38). Three thousand gladly received the way of salvation, repented, and were baptized for the forgiveness of sins (Acts 2:38, 41).

Notice how Luke described what took place on that day. He first described the converts in terms of what they *had become* (Acts 2:41). Those who were obedient to the Word of the Lord were made into the Lord's church. They became part of a fellowship, a group. Second, Luke described them in terms of their *new behavior*. They had a new life in their behavior *toward God* (Acts 2:42). This body of redeemed people worshiped God and received divine apostolic instruction. They had a new life in their behavior *toward each other* (Acts 2:44, 45). They looked out after each other, by bearing, sharing, and caring—bearing each other's burdens, sharing with those in need, and caring for each other. This body of believers is referred to later in Acts as "the church" (Acts 5:11).

When these redeemed ones in Jerusalem came together to worship God, they were "the church" (in the assembled sense). All the redeemed in Jerusalem could be referred to as "the church in Jerusalem" (in the local sense). As that church grew and spread, all the redeemed people in the world at that time could be referred to by saying, "When Jesus comes again, He is going to receive His church (in the universal sense) and take it to heaven."

A LIVING ORGANISM

Second, we need to see the church as a living organism.

Some think of the group of saved people called "the church" as an organization, as some kind of human club. They view it as something one joins or pledges himself to, and nothing more.

As a body of redeemed people, the church is a living organism, not a human organization. The church which Christ established is living and vibrant with God's life and blessings; it is not a manmade group which is energized completely by man's wisdom, designs, and activities.

Paul described the church at Corinth as the temple, the sanctuary, or the dwelling place of God. "Do you not know that you are a temple of God, and that the Spirit of God dwells in you?" he said in 1 Corinthians

3:16.[3] Later, in 1 Corinthians 6:19, 20, Paul pictured the individual Christian as the temple of God as he condemned fornication as a sin against a person's body. First Corinthians 3:16 is a reference to the church, not the individual Christian.[4] Paul was affirming that God dwells among His people. He dwells in His people individually (1 Corinthians 6:19, 20) and collectively (1 Corinthians 3:16). In Old Testament times, God's dwelling place was the tabernacle in the wilderness and later the temple in Jerusalem; but in the Christian Age, according to Paul, God dwells in His church, His people.

The church can be likened to a living building. As Paul was illustrating what the Ephesian Christians had become, he said that they comprised a building which was made up of Christians and was in a constant stage of growth. Paul said, "In whom the whole building, being fitted together is growing into a holy temple in the Lord; in whom you also are being built together into a dwelling of God in the Spirit" (Ephesians 2:21, 22). The building he described rests upon the foundation of the apostles and prophets, with Christ Himself being the chief cornerstone. The superstructure of the building is made up of Christians. The building has no top or roof; it continually ascends upward as people obey the gospel and are added to it.

The church, then, is not an organization—it is a

---

[3]The Greek language has two words for "temple": *naos* and *hieron*. The word Paul uses for "temple" in this passage is *naos*, not *hieron*. *Naos* refers to the temple proper, the sanctuary, not the temple complex as does the word *hieron*. Paul is affirming that the body of Christ is the dwelling place of God.

[4]In this sentence, the "you" is second person plural in the Greek text, indicating that a group of people are under consideration, not just an individual as in 1 Corinthians 6:19, 20.

living organism inhabited by the Spirit of God. It is a body of Christians who are alive with the life of God and who form a dwelling place for God's Spirit. You could say that the church is God's earthly residence.

AN INTIMATE RELATIONSHIP

Third, the church should be thought of as an intimate relationship with Christ.

From the earthly viewpoint, it would be easy to think of membership in the church in terms of entering a special relationship with a group of people, with the people who make up the church. This view of the church, however, misses a significant truth. The church involves a vital, intimate, ongoing relationship, to be sure, but that relationship centers on an intimate relationship with *Jesus*.

This relationship which the church sustains to Jesus actually is so close to Him that it is described as a body/head relationship, with Christians being the body and Jesus being the head. God has made the church the spiritual body of Christ, the visible part of the invisible Christ on earth today. As surely as the Lord while on earth needed a physical body in which to accomplish His work of redemption, He now needs a spiritual body in which the fruit of His redemptive work can be made available to everyone, everywhere. On the first Day of Pentecost, therefore, fifty days after His resurrection from the dead, the Holy Spirit descended to form the church, that spiritual body of Christ. From that day until this, every redeemed person, at the time of His redemption, is placed by the wondrous grace of God in that body.

Thus, the church in the New Testament is commonly called by the inspired writers "the body of

Christ" (Ephesians 1:21, 22; 5:23). Those who obey the gospel of Christ become, and literally function as, Christ's spiritual body on earth, led by the head, Christ Himself. So true is this that when one is baptized, the New Testament specifically says that he is baptized "into Christ" or "into His body" (Romans 6:3; 1 Corinthians 12:13; Galatians 3:27).

As a body of redeemed people,
the church is a living organism,
not a human organization.

The church has the closest relationship to Jesus into which a person can enter upon this earth. The church is the fullness of Christ, for His body is the fullness of Him who fills all in all (Ephesians 1:23), and Christ is the fullness of the church, for we are complete in Him (Colossians 2:10). The church, His body, is incomplete without Christ, the head (Ephesians 1:22); and Christ, the head, is incomplete without His body, the church (Colossians 1:18). All that the head of the church is and has is the possession of the church, and all that the church is and has is the possession of Christ, our head. As His church, therefore, we experience a daily, continual partnership with Jesus. In Christ, we are not just professors of Christianity; we are possessors of Christ. In His body, the fountain of the fullness of Christ is open to us.

As Paul discussed the church in Ephesians 5, he compared its relationship to Christ by using the figure of the husband/wife relationship, with the husband illustrating Christ and the wife illustrating the church. He referred to this relationship first *in principle*. Christ is the head of the church even as the husband is the head of the wife (Ephesians 5:23). He spoke of this relationship second *in practice or function*. As the wife is to be subject to her husband in everything, even so the church is to be subject to Christ. It is to look to Jesus as its head, leader, and guide (Ephesians 5:24). Finally, Paul discussed this relationship *in purpose*. As a husband loves his wife, Christ loves the church and is preparing this body of believers in Him to live with Him in eternity (Ephesians 5:25-27).

The church of the New Testament, at its heart, is a relationship with Christ. It is not initially a relationship with people, but it immediately results in a relationship with other Christians, the other members of the church, even as the children of the same father are secondarily related to each other. Members of Christ's body are members of each other, but, first and foremost, the church is Christ's body. To be members of Christ's church we must enter a relationship with Christ, a relationship so intimate and special that we are part of Him even as a body belongs to the head.

CONCLUSION

Many are confused on the proper meaning of the word "church." Such confusion need not exist, for the Bible is clear on its meaning.

What is "the church"? It is a spiritual body made up of those who have obeyed the gospel of Christ, have become His people, and are worshiping and working as His people in a given community. They wear His name and are His spiritual body on earth. They honor Christ in all things. This spiritual body is a living organism in which dwells the Spirit of the living God; it is not a human organization. It is not just membership in a group. It is an intimate, ongoing relationship with Christ.

The church, the body of Christ, is entered by faith. This faith response involves repentance (Acts 17:30, 31), confession of Jesus as God's Son (Romans 10:10), and baptism into Christ (Romans 6:3; Galatians 3:27). At the point of baptism, one's sins are washed away and, with his new birth completed, he becomes a part of the body of Christ (Acts 2:38, 41, 47; 22:16; 1 Corinthians 12:13).

The church of the New Testament is not a denomination. Denominations are manmade; the church in the New Testament is designed, created, indwelt, and sustained by the Lord. Denominations come from the earth, from man; the New Testament church comes from heaven, from God. The church belongs to Christ— it wears His name, meets together for His worship, does His work in the world, and is indwelt by His Spirit.

The invitation is extended by Christ to all men to enter His church upon His terms of salvation (Revelation 22:17) and live in the world as His church.

QUESTIONS FOR STUDY
AND DISCUSSION

1. Think of a time in your personal experience when a failure on your part to notice how a word or phrase was being used by another person resulted in a breakdown in communication. Relate the instance.

2. Discuss the significance of the context in understanding a given verse of Scripture. Is the meaning of various words indicated by the context?

3. How necessary is it to ascertain how the Holy Spirit is using a word in the Scriptures? Relate this importance to His use of the word "church" in the New Testament.

4. Give a simple but complete definition of the word "church" as this word is used in the New Testament.

5. Discuss the different ways the word "church" is used in the New Testament, and give examples of each use.

6. Apply the different uses of the word "church" to those who became Christians on the Day of Pentecost in Acts 2.

7. What implications does the truth that the church is the temple of God have for our lives today? Does this designation suggest how we are to live, work, and worship?

8. In what sense is the church a "living" building?

9. What does the "body" concept suggest about the nature of the church?

10. In what ways can the husband/wife relationship illustrate the church's relationship to Jesus?

11. Describe clearly how one enters Christ's church.

12. In what sense does the church uniquely belong to Christ?

2

The Bible's Big Beginning

"So then, those who had received his word were baptized; and there were added that day about three thousand souls" (Acts 2:41).

When a professor counsels a student on how to read a chapter of a book for an assignment, he usually says, "Look for pivotal points or crucial ideas which are the roots of the author's thoughts and give rise to his other ideas." This method is not only good advice for reading almost any book; it is also sound guidance for reading *the* book, the Bible.

For serious Bible study, the message of the Bible should be placed within a framework of pivotal turning points or around the crucial root ideas of God's truth. Every line of the Bible is God's inspired Word and is important to us; we must not denigrate any part of it. We cannot understand the truths of the Bible, however, unless we place them in their appropriate contexts. Preachers, a number of years ago, would say that we must "rightly divide the Bible." They taught people to see the Bible in connection with its age divisions, or periods of its history, warning them that a failure to recognize these divisions of the Patriarchal, Mosaical, and Christian Ages would lead to a misinterpretation and misapplication of the Bible to their lives. Their words constitute wise instruction that certainly needs to be heeded by the diligent student of the Bible.

Let us apply this truth of "rightly dividing the Bible" to the Old Testament and the early part of the New Testament. The Old Testament abounds with prophetic fingers pointing to a major event yet to come in the distant future called "the last days." The event would begin with the Messiah's coming and would coalesce into *the* major event that would be the very fulfillment of the Savior's coming.

In the first five books of the New Testament, six major junctures or turning points are evident: (1) the birth of Jesus, (2) the preparatory preaching of John, (3) the baptism and temptations of Jesus, (4) the ministry of Jesus, (5) Jesus' death and resurrection, and (6) the beginning of the church/kingdom. The first five junctures actually lay the foundation for the sixth juncture. In essence, Matthew, Mark, Luke, and John prepare the way for the establishment of the kingdom of heaven, the church. These four books culminate in the Acts 2 story of the beginning of the church.

Judging, then, from the very movement of the Old and New Testament story—the movement from the prophets to the birth of Jesus to the fullness-of-time for the bringing in of the church—it is evident that the beginning of the church is the high point of significance in the narrative that is unfolded in the Old and New Testaments.

In light of the attention given in both testaments to the beginning of the church or the kingdom, God must have wanted us to consider carefully the paramount nature of this event. Let us look at the background of the setting up of the church with the hope of understanding it better and appreciating it more.

THE BIG BEGINNING PROPHESIED

The church was not an afterthought or an accident in the mind of God. From eternity past, it was part of the divine purpose of God. Long before the New Testament days, it was spoken of by the prophets as the coming kingdom of God.

One of the great prophecies foretelling the establishment of the church is found in Daniel 2:36-44. Nebuchadnezzar had seen a great image in a dream. Its head was made of gold, its arms and chest were of silver, its belly and thighs were of brass, and its feet and toes were of iron mixed with clay. The dream troubled Nebuchadnezzar so much that he was unable to sleep. He sought the interpretation of the dream from his magicians and sorcerers, but the interpretation eluded them. Eventually, Daniel, God's prophet, was brought before him to interpret the dream. By God's power, Daniel revealed to Nebuchadnezzar God's purpose in the dream. Daniel's interpretation makes it clear that the dream and the interpretation are not just for Nebuchadnezzar but for the larger audience of the readers of the Book of Daniel, for the dream foretells the coming of the kingdom of God.

Daniel said that Nebuchadnezzar, as a world ruler and the head of the Babylonian Empire, was the head of gold (Daniel 2:38). After Nebuchadnezzar, three other world kingdoms were to arise. The arms and chest of the image represented the Medo-Persian Empire, the next world empire after Babylon. The belly and thighs symbolized the Grecian Empire, which was created by Alexander the Great and was the third world empire. The final part of the image illustrated the Roman Empire, which was established by Caesar Augustus in 31 B.C. and was the fourth world empire of the dream.

The Roman Empire came to an end around 476 years after the birth of Christ. Therefore, Daniel's prophecy said that sometime between 31 B.C. and A.D. 476, during the days of the Roman kings, the God of heaven would set up His kingdom: "And in the days of those kings the God of heaven will set up a kingdom which will never be destroyed, and that kingdom will not be left for another people; it will crush and put an end to all these kingdoms, but it will itself endure forever" (Daniel 2:44).

Daniel's interpretation pointed to a time, four or five hundred years in the future from his day, when the church or God's kingdom would be established. God's kingdom would exist on earth as these four world kingdoms had, but God's kingdom would endure and not come to an end as the four world kingdoms had. It would be eternal. The content of this prophecy reminds us of the words of Christ as He anticipated the establishment of His church: "And I also say to you that you are Peter, and upon this rock I will build My church; and the gates of Hades shall not overpower it" (Matthew 16:18).

Repeated emphasis suggests importance. Any communiqué that repeatedly emphasizes a certain thought or command is to be understood as conveying significance through its repetition. The fact that the church is the subject of numerous Old Testament prophecies indicates that the church is part of God's eternal purpose and the object of His emphasis and special importance. The church should be very special to us since it is of foremost importance to God.

THE BIG BEGINNING PLANNED

The coming of the church was intricately planned. Christ's major work during His ministry was to lay the foundation for His kingdom or church.

Nothing should be more heart-lifting to any of us than the truth that the Lord's church was established according to the plan of our blessed Lord.

John's ministry could be designated as *preparational*. He prepared the way for the ministry of Christ. His preaching sounded two characteristic themes: "Repent, for the kingdom of heaven is at hand" (Matthew 3:2) and "He who is coming after me is mightier than I" (Matthew 3:11). "At hand" meant "near" or "not far away." As the people listened to John, their hearts began to beat with anticipation concerning the coming of the Messiah and the coming of the kingdom of God. Although John's ministry lasted probably no longer than a year, he, as a voice crying in the wilderness, as an advance runner heralding the coming of the king, laid the groundwork for the ministry of Christ.

Christ's ministry could be called *foundational*. He was born under the law of Moses, and He lived His entire life under it; but in His example and precepts He taught men how they were to live under the special rule of God when the kingdom of God came. His sermons, conversations, and ministry priorities were keyed to laying the foundation for the coming of the kingdom.

To one gathering of people, Christ said, "Truly I say to you, there are some of those who are standing here who shall not taste death until they see the kingdom of God after it has come with power" (Mark 9:1). At this point in time, the kingdom's coming was very near, even within the lifetime of some who were listening to Him. Christ even identified the way the kingdom would come—"with power."

After His resurrection, Christ said,

> Thus it is written, that the Christ should suffer and rise again from the dead the third day; and that repentance for forgiveness of sins should be proclaimed in His name to all the nations, beginning from Jerusalem. You are witnesses of these things. And behold, I am sending forth the promise of My Father upon you; but you are to stay in the city until you are clothed with power from on high (Luke 24:46-49).

In His statement, Christ also named the place of the coming of the power—Jerusalem. The coming of the kingdom was approaching, and the place where it would begin was Jerusalem.

On the day of His ascension, Christ said to His apostles, "But you shall receive power when the Holy Spirit has come upon you; and you shall be My witnesses both in Jerusalem, and in all Judea and Samaria, and even to the remotest part of the earth" (Acts 1:8). Thus, the power that would accompany the coming of the kingdom would come when the Holy Spirit came upon the apostles.

Four facts are evident from these statements of Christ: (1) At the time He spoke, the establishment of the church or kingdom was not far away, (2) the establishment of the church or kingdom would occur at Jerusalem, (3) the establishment of the kingdom would be accompanied by power, and (4) the apostles would receive that power when the Holy Spirit was poured out upon them.

The foundation is vital in building any kind of physical house. The bigger or the more enduring the house is intended to be, the more important the foundation becomes. Christ used His entire ministry to lay the foundation for the establishment of the church. The extensive preparation which was made for the church or kingdom suggests how important the church is to God and how critical it is to mankind.

THE BIG EVENT PICTURED

When was the church actually established? When were the prophecies concerning the church fulfilled? When were the plans which were made for it finally realized?

Prior to the Day of Pentecost, the church or kingdom is always spoken of in the future tense; it is always something coming. From Pentecost forward, however, it is spoken of in the present tense; it is a reality—it has come.

Within Acts 2 are recorded the circumstances and events which fulfill all the Old and New Testament predictions regarding the establishment of the eternal kingdom. Acts 2 qualifies as the fulfillment of Daniel 2:44, for it falls within the time span foretold by

Daniel—that time span indicated by the phrase "in the days of these kings." Mark 9:1 is fulfilled in Acts 2, for some of those present when Jesus uttered His statement about the coming kingdom were present on Pentecost. For example, the apostles heard His statement in Mark 9:1 and were present on Pentecost. Luke 24:46-49 is fulfilled in Acts 2, for the setting of Acts 2 is Jerusalem. Acts 1:6-8 is fulfilled in Acts 2, for the Holy Spirit descends (Acts 2:1-4) upon the apostles and they receive the power that had been promised. Undoubtedly, Acts 2 pictures the establishment of the church or kingdom of God. Hence, from Acts 2 forward, the church is spoken of as being in existence (Acts 8:1, 3; 9:31; 11:22; Colossians 1:13).

After the apostles were baptized with the Holy Spirit on the Day of Pentecost, they preached the gospel of the resurrected Christ to those who had gathered. Peter preached the principal sermon, which is often called the first gospel sermon to be preached after the Great Commission was given. He presented the evidence which proved that Jesus whom they had crucified had been made both Lord and Christ (Acts 2:36). Convicted by this evidence, many cried out, "What shall we do?" (Acts 2:37). Peter told these believers to repent and be baptized for the forgiveness of sins (Acts 2:38). Those who opened their hearts to his inspired words repented and were baptized. Three thousand were baptized that day (Acts 2:41). The church of our Lord was thus established. The kingdom of God had come. In the remaining part of Acts 2, the daily, ongoing life of the church is described (Acts 2:42-47).

God's Word provides the testimony for true faith. Paul said, "So faith comes from hearing, and hearing by the word of Christ" (Romans 10:17). If you cannot read about it in the Bible, you cannot believe in it with biblical faith. Authentic faith is not a "blind leap into the dark"; it is an informed commitment to following God's Word. If you cannot read it, do not receive it. Any God-sent revival is based upon the God-inspired Bible.

Can you read of the establishment of the church of which you are a member in Acts 2? Is your religion based upon human supposition or divine Scripture?

CONCLUSION

How priceless and precious the church or kingdom must be to God! Through numerous prophecies of the Old Testament, God stresses the importance of the coming of the kingdom. In addition, He shows the importance of the church to Him in the emphasis which is given in the Gospels to laying a foundation for it by the earthly ministry of Jesus. Then, immediately following our Lord's resurrection and ascension, God depicts the value of the church by picturing the outpouring of the Holy Spirit and the actual establishment of His kingdom as three thousand souls are brought into it.

Nothing should be more heart-lifting to any of us than the truth that the Lord's church was established according to the plan of our blessed Lord. The church the Lord promised is in existence now and will continue forever.

The church is the most consequential kingdom into which people can enter. Members of it are blessed beyond measure, having access to all spiritual blessings (Ephesians 1:3) and possessing eternal life (1 John 5:13). Those who do not take advantage of their opportunity to enter the kingdom of God surely have failed to understand its significance. No earthly kingdom is comparable to it. It is spiritual in nature, eternal in quality, and divine in origin. No wonder the church can only be entered by a new birth (John 3:5).

QUESTIONS FOR STUDY AND DISCUSSION

1. Give a simple definition of the phrase "rightly dividing the Bible."
2. List the six major junctures of the first five books of the New Testament.
3. Why should we consider the establishment of the church as a high point in Bible history?
4. Explain the dream that Nebuchadnezzar had in the days of Daniel.
5. What interpretation did Daniel give to Nebuchadnezzar's dream?
6. When did Daniel say that the God of heaven would set up His kingdom?
7. According to Daniel, what kind of duration would the kingdom of heaven have?
8. As John prepared the people for the coming of Christ, what two notes did he sound?
9. In what sense was the ministry of Christ foundational?
10. What implications regarding time does Mark 9:1 have for the coming of the kingdom?
11. Discuss this phrase uttered by Christ concerning the coming of the kingdom: "You shall receive power when the Holy Spirit has come upon you."
12. Discuss how Acts 2 fulfills all the prophecies concerning the coming of the kingdom.
13. What kind of assurance does the realization that the church has been established bring to us?

3

The Day the Church Came, 1

"And when the day of Pentecost had come, they were all together in one place" (Acts 2:1).
"And suddenly there came from heaven a noise like a violent, rushing wind, . . ." (Acts 2:2).
"But Peter, taking his stand with the eleven, raised his voice and declared to them: . . ." (Acts 2:14).

In 1965, the United Artists Corporation released a film on the life of Christ which was called *The Greatest Story Ever Told*. Beginning with Christ's birth, the movie depicts His earthly ministry, rejection, crucifixion, burial, and resurrection. Although the production of the movie was not faithful to the divine record of the Bible in its portrayal of Jesus, its title does remind us that the actual life of Christ is the greatest story ever told.

If the birth, life, death, and resurrection of Jesus is the greatest story ever told, what would be the next-to-the-greatest story ever told, the sequel to the greatest story ever told? The answer is obvious as one reads

35

the Book of Acts in the New Testament: The continuation to the greatest story ever told is the establishment of our Lord's church.

This story of the bringing in of the kingdom of God, the church, as one would expect, is filled with high adventure and gripping excitement. One chapter in Acts—chapter 2—relates the drama.

Let us review this chapter in Acts as if this one chapter were an entire book or a complete story. This will allow us to divide the story into its compelling and inspiring parts. Each chapter in the book *The Sequel to the Greatest Story Ever Told* will present an intriguing phase of the story of the establishment of the church.

THE DIVINE OUTPOURING

As we begin the book, we open to the first chapter, which is entitled "The Divine Outpouring."

Luke, the writer of Acts, says, "And when the day of Pentecost had come, they were all together in one place." The setting of the story, therefore, is the historic city of Jerusalem on the Day of Pentecost. Isaiah (Isaiah 2:2-4) and Micah (Micah 4:1-3) had prophetically marked Jerusalem as the place where the law of the Lord would go forth in the beginning of the age called "the last days." Pentecost was an Old Testament feast day which celebrated the harvest of grain (Exodus 23:16). From all over the Roman Empire, Jewish men with their families had come to Jerusalem to keep this important Old Testament festival.

As the Day of Pentecost was getting fully under way, Luke records,

And suddenly there came from heaven a noise like

a violent, rushing wind, and it filled the whole house where they were sitting. And there appeared to them tongues as of fire distributing themselves, and they rested on each one of them. And they were all filled with the Holy Spirit and began to speak with other tongues, as the Spirit was giving them utterance (Acts 2:2-4).

That only the apostles were the recipients of the outpouring of the Holy Spirit is evident from the record within Acts 2 and from the context leading up to Acts 2. First, the pronoun "they" of Acts 2:1 modifies "the eleven apostles" of Acts 1:26. Accordingly, the apostles are the center of attention as the story unfolds. Second, the account of the coming of the Holy Spirit (Acts 2:1-21) nowhere indicates that anyone other than the apostles received the baptism of the Holy Spirit. The multitude that witnessed the apostles' speaking in different languages through the Spirit recognized and acknowledged only the apostles as the ones doing the speaking (Acts 2:7).

For three years prior to this outpouring of the Holy Spirit, the apostles received promises in different circumstances about how Christ would one day baptize them with the Holy Spirit. At the beginning of Christ's ministry, John the Baptist had said, "As for me, I baptize you with water for repentance; but He who is coming after me is mightier than I, and I am not fit to remove His sandals; He will baptize you with the Holy Spirit and fire" (Matthew 3:11). Shortly before His ascension, Christ had said to them, "For John baptized with water, but you shall be baptized with the Holy Spirit not many days from now" (Acts 1:5). The parting words of Christ to His apostles at His ascension, instructed them to abide in Jerusalem until they had received the promise of the Father and were clothed with power from on high (Luke 24:46-49; Acts 1:4). Now, in this divine outpouring of the Holy Spirit which came on the morning of the Day of Pentecost, all of our Lord's promises concerning the coming of the Spirit upon the apostles were being fulfilled.

The apostles were baptized with the Holy Spirit for three divine purposes.

As the Holy Spirit was poured out from heaven, something was heard: ". . . there came from heaven a noise like a violent, rushing wind, . . ." (Acts 2:2). Something was also seen: "And there appeared to them tongues as of fire distributing themselves, and they rested on each one of them" (Acts 2:3). Something was also experienced: The outward manifestation of the coming of the Spirit was the apostles' speaking in tongues, or languages, as the Spirit empowered them. There can be no doubt that the apostles were speaking in the human languages of the people who had heard the sound resembling wind and had gathered to see what was happening. As the people spoke of what they were hearing from the apostles, they used the Greek words *dialektos* (translated "language"; Acts 2:6, 8) and *glossais* (translated "tongue"; Acts 2:11).

The apostles were baptized with the Holy Spirit for three divine purposes. First, they were baptized for the purpose of *inspiration*. The Holy Spirit would inspire them so they could give God's revelation to the world. Christ had promised the apostles, "But the

Helper, the Holy Spirit, whom the Father will send in My name, He will teach you all things, and bring to your remembrance all that I said to you" (John 14:26). Now, through the coming of the Spirit, this promise of inspiration that Christ had made to His apostles would be realized.

Second, they were baptized with the Holy Spirit for the purpose of *confirmation*. They would be empowered by the Holy Spirit to work miracles, signs, and wonders to confirm or authenticate the messages they would preach. Christ had promised, "And these signs will accompany those who have believed: in My name they will cast out demons, they will speak with new tongues; they will pick up serpents, and if they drink any deadly poison, it shall not hurt them; they will lay hands on the sick, and they will recover" (Mark 16:17, 18). This promise would be fulfilled through the Spirit as the apostles worked miracles to confirm that they were men sent from God. An illustration of its fulfillment is seen in Acts 14:3: "Therefore they spent a long time there speaking boldly with reliance upon the Lord, who was bearing witness to the word of His grace, granting that signs and wonders be done by their hands."

Third, they were baptized with the Holy Spirit for the purpose of *impartation*. By the empowerment of the Spirit, they were enabled to lay hands on other Christians and impart to them the miraculous gifts of the Holy Spirit. An example of this impartation is recorded in Acts 8:14-24: Peter and John, two apostles, were sent out from Jerusalem to Samaria to pray for the new converts who had come to Christ through Philip's preaching. They also laid hands on the Christians and imparted miraculous gifts of the Holy Spirit to them.

What does this first part of the "next-to-the-greatest story ever told" mean to you and me? It means that the revelation found in the New Testament was given to us through inspired men. We can trust the New Testament message to be accurate and infallible. God empowered His apostles through the baptism of the Holy Spirit; and the apostles, in turn, by the laying on of their hands, imparted miraculous gifts of the Holy Spirit to other Christians. Thus, all the New Testament writers were inspired, Spirit-guided men. All of which means that we can believe confidently that the New Testament is God's revelation to man.

THE DISTRACTED MULTITUDE

Chapter two of *The Sequel to the Greatest Story Ever Told* is entitled "The Distracted Multitude." The city of Jerusalem was thronging with people on this special day, the Day of Pentecost, and many of those people who had come to keep this feast would be privileged to be present when the church came into existence.

> Now there were Jews living in Jerusalem, devout men, from every nation under heaven. . . . "Parthians and Medes and Elamites, and residents of Mesopotamia, Judea and Cappadocia, Pontus and Asia, Phrygia and Pamphylia, Egypt and the districts of Libya around Cyrene, and visitors from Rome, both Jews and proselytes, Cretans and Arabs—we hear them in our own tongues speaking of the mighty deeds of God" (Acts 2:5-11).

Luke described visitors in Jerusalem who had traveled to Jerusalem from at least fifteen different areas of the Roman Empire.

The people who had been drawn together by the sound of the rushing mighty wind were Jews, and thus provided an audience of unusual potential for this first preaching of the gospel. They had a *mental potential*. They were believers in God and knew well the Old Testament Scriptures. They had an intellectual readiness for the reception of the gospel message.

They also had a *missionary potential*. They could return to their homelands with the gospel that they had heard. The people had come from all over the Roman Empire. The opportunity was present for an immediate spread of Christianity by these people who would receive the gospel and would later return to their communities with it.

You could say that there are two parts to a song: the one who sings it and the one who listens to it. If you have only the singing of song and no one to hear it, the one who sings it might be benefited by singing it, but the value of the song goes no further. The same is true of preaching. The preacher does and should preach to himself, but he really builds his sermon for the congregation, those who are going to hear it.

The quality of the audience makes a big difference in public speaking. After a sermon is delivered, two evaluations should be made: one of the preacher and one of the congregation. We have to ask, "Was the sermon true to the Word of God and delivered in the spirit of Christ? Did the congregation listen to the preaching as honest hearers?

Some in this large multitude that gathered were ready to listen. When they were given an opportunity to see the evidence anew and afresh, they would receive it.

THE DISARMING INTRODUCTION

The day on which the church was established was

a day of preaching. At first, apparently all the apostles spoke to the different ethnic and national groups in their languages or dialects, declaring "the mighty deeds of God" (Acts 2:11). Then Peter stood up with the eleven and delivered a detailed sermon, speaking perhaps in Greek, a universal language of that day, proclaiming that Jesus was both Lord and Christ (Acts 2:14).

Through inspiration, Luke provides us with a summary of the sermon Peter preached (Acts 2:14-36). This vital overview he gave of Peter's sermon can be outlined in two or three different ways; but let us outline it according to the formal elements of a typical speech, looking at its introduction, body, and conclusion.

---

*God would use the miraculous
gifts of the Spirit . . . until
the written form of the
New Testament appeared.*

Peter began the sermon by starting where his audience was. Some of the people had mockingly said, "They are full of sweet wine" (Acts 2:13). Preachers of the gospel can get along without just about anything except a good reputation. Any preacher who does not have trustworthy character and a reliable reputation is doomed to failure before he opens his mouth to speak. He will not be believed or respected regardless of how eloquent his presentation of the gospel may be.

It is no surprise, then, that Peter began this sermon with an answer to the accusation that had been made against the apostles. He responded to their distortion of what had happened with two affirmations: First, he affirmed what it was not. He appealed to their common sense. He said, "For these men are not drunk, as you suppose, for it is only the third hour of the day" (Acts 2:15). Peter was saying, "The explanation of this phenomenon cannot be drunkenness, for no normal Jew would be intoxicated so early in the morning on such an important day as Pentecost. Common sense will tell you that we are not intoxicated." Second, Peter affirmed what it was. He appealed to Scripture as he said, "But this is what was spoken of through the prophet Joel" (Acts 2:16). He then proceeded to quote Joel 2:28-32 (Acts 2:17-21). Thus, there can be no doubt that the outpouring of the Spirit on Pentecost is, at least in part, the fulfillment of Joel's prophecy regarding the beginning of the age called "the last days." We have Peter's word on it. His words, "This is what was spoken of through the prophet Joel," must be regarded as a definitive and final answer to this question.

This outpouring of the Spirit began the age of "the last days." As the apostles were empowered by the baptism of the Holy Spirit, the miraculous age of the beginning of the church commenced. Later in Acts, the apostles laid their hands upon other Christians, and sons and daughters prophesied, young men saw visions, old men dreamed dreams, and men and women bondservants prophesied (Acts 6:6; 8:4-8, 14-24; 21:8, 9). This outpouring upon the apostles was the fountainhead which produced the miraculous stream of the early days of Christianity. God would use the miraculous gifts of the Spirit imparted by the laying on of apostolic hands for the guidance of the infant church until the written form of the New Testament appeared. With the completion of the written form of the New Testament and the deaths of the apostles and the deaths of those on whom the apostles had laid their hands, the age of the miraculous beginning of the church ended and the age of the Spirit guiding the church through the written Word commenced.

Peter's introduction, then, pointed out to the multitude what the event was not and what the event was. He appealed to their common sense, and he appealed to Scripture. He took his audience from where they were to where they would be ready to consider the evidence for Jesus' being the Messiah.

THE DYNAMIC ARGUMENT

The body of his sermon consists of a presentation of different lines of evidence for believing that Jesus is the Christ. If you were asked to stand before an assembly of thousands of people and list the evidence for believing that Jesus is the Christ, what evidence would you list? Let us see what evidence he gave and check our list against his.

When the repetition is eliminated, Peter listed and explained five lines of evidence. First, he pointed to the evidence of *the miracles of Christ*. He said, ". . . Jesus the Nazarene, a man attested to you by God with miracles and wonders and signs which God performed through Him in your midst, just as you yourselves know—" (Acts 2:22). It was the testimony of the miracles that had convinced Nicodemus that Christ had come from God. During his night interview with Christ, Nicodemus said, "Rabbi, we know that You have come from God as a teacher; for no one can do these signs that You do unless God is with him" (John 3:2). If a completely credible source of information, an undeniably reliable document, declared to us that Jesus worked true miracles, we would be forced by that testimony to respond to the miracles of Christ the same way that

Nicodemus did—we would be compelled to believe that He came from God. The Word of God, the Bible, the most reliable source of information on earth, testifies that Christ worked actual miracles. This evidence can point to only one conclusion—He was "approved" of God, confirmed by the miracles He worked as being God's Son. Peter reminded his audience of the miracles of Christ and called for an acceptance of the logical conclusion which that evidence demands.

Second, Peter placed before his audience the evidence of *the resurrection*. He said,

> This Man, delivered up by the predetermined plan and foreknowledge of God, you nailed to a cross by the hands of godless men and put Him to death. And God raised Him up again, putting an end to the agony of death, since it was impossible for Him to be held in its power (Acts 2:23, 24).

The resurrection was a significant part of all apostolic preaching. It was an argument that the Jews could not answer. The resurrection of Christ made cowards out of bold men and made bold men out of cowards. The Jews who had boldly cried before Pilate, "Let Him be crucified!" (Matthew 27:22) were cringing in fear before the truth of the empty tomb. Peter, who had fearfully said at Christ's trial, "I do not know the man" (Matthew 26:72), was boldly preaching His resurrection before a vast assembly only a short distance from the empty tomb.

The resurrection provides conclusive proof that Jesus Christ is God's Son. The only way anyone can deny the deity of Christ is to deny His resurrection from the dead. The resurrection places Christianity in a category all by itself. Christianity is the only religion in the world of religions whose founder arose from the dead. It confirms His claims, authenticates His promises, and validates His religion.

Third, Peter argued from *the evidence of prophecy.* He quoted Psalm 16:8-11, a prophecy which predicted the resurrection of Christ:

> I was always beholding the Lord in my presence; for He is at my right hand, that I may not be shaken. Therefore my heart was glad and my tongue exulted; moreover my flesh also will abide in hope; because Thou wilt not abandon my soul to Hades, nor allow Thy Holy One to undergo decay. Thou hast made known to me the ways of life; Thou wilt make me full of gladness with Thy presence (Acts 2:25-28).

In his prophecy, David spoke in the first person. On the surface, it might appear that he was speaking of himself. Peter showed that David could not have been speaking of himself by pointing to two facts. First, he referred to David's death. He said that David, the one who made the prophecy, died and was buried and was still in his tomb. As his evidence, he pointed to David's tomb, which was located in Jerusalem for all to see (Acts 2:29). Second, he reminded them of God's promise to David (Acts 2:30). God had promised David that one of his descendants would eventually come and occupy his throne (2 Samuel 7:12). This promise, Peter said, has been fulfilled in Christ, for God has raised Him from the dead (Acts 2:31), placing Him at His right hand on a spiritual throne. Jesus came into the world through the lineage of David and now sits on a spiritual throne at God's right hand in heaven, reigning as King over His earthly kingdom, the church.

Peter made a similar argument from a prophecy in

Psalm 110:1 at the end of his sermon (Acts 2:34, 35). His references to prophecy (Psalms 16:8-11; 110:1) proved that the One sent from God would be resurrected from the dead and exalted to God's right hand. Jesus, in His resurrection and exaltation, had clearly fulfilled both of these Old Testament prophecies.

Fourth, Peter used *the evidence of witnesses.* He said, "This Jesus God raised up again, to which we are all witnesses" (Acts 2:32). The Jews would have to acknowledge that the prophecy to which Peter had referred predicted a resurrection. Peter was seeking to confirm that Christ had arisen from the dead and had fulfilled that part of the prophecy. He forced his audience to face the testimony of eyewitnesses that Jesus had arisen from the dead. A witness is high-quality evidence. Any authentic court of law will accept the evidence of a witness as long as no contradictions are evident in his testimony. God not only affirmed the resurrection of His Son in His Word, but He placed in His Word the testimony of witnesses who, after His resurrection from the dead, saw Him, touched Him, ate with Him, and studied Him. Who could refuse such testimony?

Fifth, Peter pointed to the evidence of *the descent of the Spirit.* He said, "Therefore having been exalted to the right hand of God, and having received from the Father the promise of the Holy Spirit, He has poured forth this which you both see and hear" (Acts 2:33). Just before Christ's departure to heaven, He promised to send the promise of the Father to the apostles (Luke 24:46-49). The multitude had seen and heard the results of the outpouring of the Spirit. Thus, they had miraculous confirmation that Jesus had ascended to the Father's right hand, had received from the Father the promise of the Spirit, and had sent the Spirit forth upon the apostles.

These five lines of evidence, these five proofs, establish an undeniable conclusion. Peter focused the attention of the audience on this conclusion with the word "therefore." Someone has said, "Whenever you see the word 'therefore' in the New Testament, you should stop and see what it is *there for*, for it is always *there for* a reason." Peter said, "Therefore let all the house of Israel know for certain that God has made Him both Lord and Christ—this Jesus whom you crucified" (Acts 2:36). His miracles, His resurrection from the dead, His fulfillment of prophecy, the testimony of witnesses, and the descent of the Spirit prove that Jesus is the promised One of God, the Christ, and that He is Lord.

His miracles, His resurrection from the dead, His fulfillment of prophecy, the testimony of witnesses, and the descent of the Spirit prove that Jesus is the promised One of God, the Christ, and that He is Lord.

What does this part of the sequel to the greatest story ever told mean to us? Does it not convince us that Christ is the center of Christianity? When one proves that Jesus is the Christ, he proves the credibility of Christianity. If Peter could not have proven that Christ was God's Son who died for our sins and arose from the dead, Christianity would have died on the day of its birth! Since Peter proved that Jesus was the Christ, he validated Christianity as the only authentic religion in the world from God.

CONCLUSION

In these first four chapters of this fascinating book, *The Sequel to the Greatest Story Ever Told*, we have seen what God did to "bring in" the church or the kingdom. Pouring out the Spirit in a baptismal measure upon the apostles, He equipped them to be part of the foundation of the church (Ephesians 2:20) and prepared them to preach infallibly His message of redemption to the world (Luke 24:46-49).

By the sounds and events that were occurring, God brought together a huge multitude as a ready audience for the first preaching of the gospel. The people were primed and prepared for a proclamation about the deity of Jesus.

Peter, the apostle to whom He had promised the keys to the kingdom (Matthew 16:19), was granted the immortal privilege of preaching the first gospel sermon of the Christian Age. By these events, God set in place the foundation of the church and gave an invitation for people to enter the church and live upon that foundation. Therefore, the long years of prophetic expectation has burst forth into a glorious fulfillment, like a homely bud erupting into a gorgeous flower.

The miraculous events of Pentecost were once-for-all-time events. They established for all Bible believers to see that the kingdom has come. Pentecost cannot be recreated, repeated, or relived. It can only be received and built upon. Anyone anywhere can enter the church that was established upon this Pentecost Day but God is not going to pour out His Holy Spirit miraculously every time a new body of the church is established in some other place in the world. There is no need for Him to provide such confirmation, for this beginning of the church stands forever, proven by the testimony of the Scriptures until the end of time.

God proclaims the "coming in" of the kingdom by one of the most attention-getting miracles of the New Testament, the miraculous outpouring of the Holy Spirit upon the apostles. He leaves no room for doubt in the mind of the sincere seeker for truth. He makes it as clear as the dazzling sun on a cloudless day.

Furthermore, God has confirmed for all time the integrity of His promises with the supernatural events of Pentecost. Had He not poured out the Spirit as He did, we would be left to wonder about the truthfulness of God and the authenticity of Christianity. By the events of Pentecost, God established Christianity as historically true, and thus as the world's only divinely-given religion. Hence, when we come to Christ properly, we come to the truth (John 14:6); when we obey the truth properly, we come to Christ (John 8:32).

The first part of our story causes us to joyfully exclaim "Christianity is wondrously true and truly wonderful!"

QUESTIONS FOR STUDY AND DISCUSSION

1. In what sense can we say that the establishment of the church is the sequel to the greatest story ever told?
2. What evidence can you give that only the apostles were baptized with the Holy Spirit on Pentecost?
3. Discuss the divine reasons that the apostles were baptized with the Holy Spirit.

4. What does the baptism of the apostles in the Holy Spirit mean to us today?
5. Discuss the evidence for the deity of Christ which Peter presented in his sermon.
6. What kind of introduction did Peter have to his sermon?
7. How vital is the resurrection of Christ to God's scheme of redemption? Could we think of Christ in any sense as being God's divine Son if He had not arisen from the dead?

4

The Day the Church Came, 2

"Now when they heard this, they were pierced to the heart, and said to Peter and the rest of the apostles, "Brethren what shall we do?" (Acts 2:37).

"... And the Lord was adding to their number day by day those who were being saved" (Acts 2:47).

God created man as a being with the power of free choice. When He made Adam, He put enough power in his heart so that he could even shut his Creator out of his life forever if he so desired. God did not want a race of robots, a multitude of mindless "yeses"; He wanted a faithful family that would choose to love and obey Him and thus choose to honor Him as their Father. Therefore, the walk with God implies two choices—one from God and one from us, God's invitation and our answer. God offers His fellowship to us, and we accept it by spiritually taking His hand.

As we continue reading the book, *The Sequel to the Greatest Story Every Told*, we are struck by the truth that salvation has two sides, a heavenly side and a human side, God's part and man's part. When both efforts come together, the fruit of God's work rises to life, salvation results, and the church is born.

In the following part of "the day the church came" we will see more of an emphasis on the response we make to God's grace as the church is created. We have seen in a large part the divine side of the creation of the church, and now, to some degree, we will see the human part.

THE DEEP-FELT CRY

So, we have come to the fifth chapter in *The Sequel to the Greatest Story Ever Told* that is entitled "The Deep-Felt Cry." Many in Peter's audience were deeply moved by his sermon. Smitten in conscience, they cried out to Peter and to the rest of the apostles.

Luke wrote, "Now when they heard this, they were pierced to the heart, and said to Peter and the rest of the apostles, 'Brethren, what shall we do?'" (Acts 2:37). The KJV says that they were "pricked in their heart." This "pricking" of the heart is not the pricking similar to the pricking of one's finger with a needle or the pricking of one's hand by a thorn. It is an expression which means something like the breaking of the heart or like an arrow being shot through the heart. This same phrase is used in a different context in Acts 7:54: "Now when they heard this, they were cut to the quick, and they began gnashing their teeth at him." In this incident the Jews reacted to Stephen's sermon with anger. Their hearts were engulfed with anger; they were pierced through with hatred. The Jews who responded to Peter's sermon, however, were overwhelmed with conviction; they were distraught with guilt.

Perhaps the people who cried out actually interrupted Peter's sermon. Interruptions are not always desirable, but this was a blessed interruption indeed. I have heard that when Rue Porter was preaching many years ago, a man interrupted his sermon with the question "Can I be baptized now?" Brother Porter stopped his preaching, looked directly at the man, and said, "My sermon can wait. If you want to be baptized, we will stop this sermon and baptize you into Christ. Then we will come back, and I will finish the sermon." An interruption of this kind would not be an intrusion but an inspiration.

Their question was infused with fervency. They did not ask nonchalantly, "What shall we do?" Their question was more like, "What in the world can we do? We are in trouble. Do we have any hope?" Their question was asked in desperate solemnity and intensity.

Look carefully at their question: "Brethren, what shall we do?" They were addressing fellow Jews, hence, their use of the word "brethren." It has a nationality connotation, not a religious one. Their question is an expression of the world's greatest question: "What must we do to be saved?" They had come to realize that before God they were in a terrible condition. They had participated in the crucifixion of the Messiah, the Savior whom God had sent into the world. Peter's sermon places his listeners' sin before them in huge, billboard-sized letters (Acts 2:23).

You have had to ask and answer many important questions in your life, but have you asked and answered according to the New Testament the question "What must I do to be saved?" Others present on the Day of Pentecost must have heard Peter's sermon and witnessed the miracles of Pentecost but turned and walked away without facing their guilt and asking this question. Sin in a person's life is a tragedy, a tragedy so great that Christ had to come into this world and die upon a cross to provide atonement for it. There is an even greater tragedy. When one refuses to face his guilt before God and seek God's solution to that guilt, he experiences the greatest tragedy of all.

THE DEFINITIVE ANSWER

The sixth chapter in this book, *The Sequel to the Greatest Story Ever Told*, is the chapter entitled "The Definitive Answer." Peter gave a straightforward answer to the convicted crowd's question: "Repent, and let each of you be baptized in the name of Jesus Christ for the forgiveness of your sins; and you shall receive the gift of the Holy Spirit" (Acts 2:38).

Shortly before His ascension, our Lord gave what we have come to call the Great Commission. Three full accounts of this commission are given in the New Testament: Matthew 28:18-20; Mark 16:15, 16; and Luke 24:46, 47. Each account has a different emphasis. Mark 16:15, 16 stresses the condition of faith. Luke 24:46, 47 emphasizes repentance and remission of sins. Matthew 28:18-20 highlights baptism. These three accounts indicate that salvation or remission of sins through God's grace was to be offered upon the three conditions of faith, repentance, and baptism. The wording of these accounts of the Great Commission leaves no doubt as to this understanding.

All three of the conditions expressed in the Great Commission are seen in Peter's answer to their question. Faith in Christ had been engendered in their hearts by Peter's sermon, and this faith prompted their crying out for instruction. Peter's answer to the Jews' question, therefore, mentions specifically repentance and baptism, the other two conditions mentioned in the Great Commission. He said, "Repent, and let each of you be baptized in the name of Jesus Christ for the forgiveness of your sins;..." (Acts 2:38). Notice where Peter placed the remission, or forgiveness, of sins in his answer. He did not promise salvation or forgiveness of sins before baptism, but after it. Peter was guided by the Holy Spirit, and the answer he gave was the Holy Spirit's answer, not his.

If any doubt exists that baptism is for the forgiveness of sins, surely Acts 22:16 forever lays this question to rest.

The answer given those who cried out is too clear to be misunderstood. In order to dodge the force and impact of this answer, some religious leaders have said that "for" in Acts 2:38 is translated from a Greek word which does not mean "in order to" but means "because of." That the Greek word *eis* is translated reliably by "for" or "in order to" is seen by comparing the numerous translations of the Bible. Pile them on top of each other—they all render the Greek word *eis* "for," "in order to," or an equivalent phrase. None render this word "because of." Peter's answer clearly places forgiveness of sins after baptism. Let God's answer to the greatest of all questions stand, and do not allow anyone to explain it away.

Someone has said that every verse in the New Testament has a twin. This is an exaggeration, but it does have some truth to it. Some New Testament

verses have twins, and when we look at the twin we
see another way of saying the same truth. What is
the twin of Acts 2:38? It is Acts 22:16. Saul had come to
Damascus seeking the answer to his question "What
shall I do, Lord?" He was a believer, for he had seen,
spoken to, and been convicted by the Lord. His penitence was indicated by the question which he asked
the Lord. He had even acknowledged the Lord, as is
also evident in his question; but he was told to go to
Damascus that he might be told what to do. He waited
in Damascus in prayer and penitence for three days
for the answer to his question. Ananias was sent to him
with the answer. What did Ananias tell him? The
answer Ananias gave him, you might say, is the twin
of Acts 2:38. He said, "And now why do you delay?
Arise, and be baptized, and wash away your sins,
calling on His name." If any doubt exists that baptism
is for the forgiveness of sins, surely Acts 22:16 forever
lays this question to rest.

A young man who was attending a private religious college once told me that his Bible professor did
not believe that baptism should be administered for
the forgiveness of sins and was teaching this doctrine
in his class. I said, "What have you done about it?" He
said, "I asked my mother what to do about it, and she
said that I should go to him after class and ask him to
explain Acts 2:38. I did. I opened my Bible to Acts 2:38,
went to him after class, and respectfully asked him to
explain it. He said that Acts 2:38 really means 'because
of' the remission of sins and not 'for' the remission of
sins. I went home and mentioned what he had told me
to my mother, and she said that I should go back and
ask him to explain Acts 22:16. So I did. I went to him
after class with my Bible open to Acts 22:16 and re-

spectfully asked him to explain this verse. Do you know what the professor said? He said that he did not try to explain that verse but would just jump over it and go on to the next verse." I thought, "At least, the professor was honest about it." Acts 22:16 cannot be explained away. It must be accepted or rejected.

Peter indicated that the answer he gave to this great question was God's answer for the Christian Dispensation, the final age of human history. He said, "For the promise is for you and your children, and for all who are far off, as many as the Lord our God shall call to Himself" (Acts 2:39). "You and your children" is an expression that refers to the Jews who would respond to the gospel, and "for all who are far off" is an expression that must refer to or include the Gentiles who would in time hear, accept, and obey the gospel. "As many as the Lord our God shall call to Himself" is a phrase which encompasses all Jews and Gentiles who would accept the gospel in the future and come to Christ. If the Gentiles are not included in the phrase "for all who are far off," they are most assuredly included in Peter's "as many as" phrase. Peter announced God's plan not only for the Day of Pentecost but for all future days of the Christian Age. He gave God's definitive answer to the question "What must I do to be saved?"

THE DREAM-LIKE RESPONSE

The seventh chapter in the book *The Sequel to the Greatest Story Ever Told* is entitled "The Dream-Like Response." Luke tells of the amazing acceptance of the first preaching of the gospel message of salvation. He says, "So then, those who had received his word were baptized; and there were added that day about three thousand souls" (Acts 2:41).

We are not told how long Peter and the other apostles preached on this morning. Peter's sermon must have been longer than a typical Sunday morning sermon of today. Luke writes, "And with many other words he solemnly testified and kept on exhorting them, saying, 'Be saved from this perverse generation!'" (Acts 2:40). Peter not only convinced them with evidence and argument; he also compelled them with testimony and exhortation.

The listening audience accepted Peter's message and acted upon it. Luke recounts, "So then, those who had received his word were baptized; and there were added that day about three thousand souls" (Acts 2:41). These people were not just hearers of the word; they became doers of it (James 1:25). They did not just listen to it; they decided to live it. One woman who was attending a religious service became ill, and she walked outside, hoping that fresh air would help her feel better. She got some fresh air and did begin to feel better. The service had not ended, so she went back in to take part in the rest of the service. She took a seat on the back pew beside a man, and she leaned over and whispered to him, "Is the sermon done?" The man whispered back, "It has been preached; it remains to be done!" The tragedy is not that we listen to sermons; the tragedy is that all most people ever do with sermons is listen to them. Some, at least, in the great multitude that heard Peter preach were not only convicted by his message but, by yielding their minds and lives to that message, were converted to Christ.

Three thousand gladly received the Word and were baptized. Before conversion can take place, one must gladly receive the Word of salvation. One of the major reasons that more people are not converted to Christ is that people do not gladly receive the Word into their hearts. The Word will always do its work if it is gladly received.

Can you imagine what it would be like to see three thousand at one time obey Christ? In one gospel meeting in which I was privileged to preach Christ, thirty came on the final day to be baptized into Christ. We were filled with joy, but we would have to multiply that day times one hundred to understand what happened on Pentecost. J. W. McGarvey has calculated that it would take twelve men almost five hours to baptize three thousand, if one allows one minute for each baptism.[1] We do not know how the apostles did it. Maybe an apostle would baptize a man and then ask him to baptize others. Regardless of how it was done, what a day it was! This was the kind of response that every gospel preacher dreams of seeing.

THE DISTINCTIVE BODY

The eighth chapter in this book is entitled "The Distinctive Body." The three thousand who were baptized into Christ are pictured by Luke as the church.

The prophets had foretold that a unique kingdom of God was coming (Daniel 2:44). John the Baptist, as he prepared the way for the coming of the Messiah, declared that the kingdom of heaven was near (Matthew 3:1, 2). During His ministry

---

[1]"But at the rate of sixty to the hour, twelve men could baptize seven hundred twenty in one hour, and three thousand in four hours and a quarter." J. W. McGarvey, *New Commentary on Acts of the Apostles* (n.p., 1992; reprint, Delight, Ark.: Gospel Light Publishing Company, n.d.), 44.

Christ Himself, the Messiah sent from God, called for repentance because the kingdom of heaven was at hand (Matthew 4:17). After His resurrection from the dead, during the forty days before His ascension, Christ spoke with the apostles and disciples about the coming kingdom (Acts 1:3). In His final words to His apostles, Christ told them to wait for what the Father had promised (Acts 1:4). Ten days after His ascension, on a Sunday morning, the long-awaited time came. With the outpouring of the Holy Spirit (Acts 2:1-4), the first preaching of the gospel after the resurrection of Christ (Acts 2:14-36), and the response of three thousand to the gospel, the church was born. Those who were washed in the blood of Christ as they obeyed the gospel were made into Christ's church. From that day until this, every time someone hears the gospel and gladly obeys it by being baptized into Christ upon his faith, repentance, and confession of Jesus as God's Son, he is added to them (Acts 2:47)—these first ones, these three thousand who came to Christ at the very beginning on Pentecost.

From Pentecost forward in Acts, the church is spoken of as a present and living reality and no longer as a promise or prophecy. Luke said at the close of Acts 2, ". . . And the Lord was adding to their number day by day those who were being saved" (Acts 2:47). At the end of Peter's second sermon recorded in Acts, Luke wrote, "But many of those who had heard the message believed; and the number of the men came to be about five thousand" (Acts 4:4). Following the deaths of Ananias and Sapphira, Luke wrote, "And great fear came upon the whole church, and upon all who heard of these things" (Acts 5:11). When a persecution grew out of Stephen's stoning, Luke said, ". . .

And on that day a great persecution arose against the church in Jerusalem; and they were all scattered throughout the regions of Judea and Samaria, except the apostles" (Acts 8:1). According to Luke, then, the church, the unique kingdom of God had come.

It is said that one day someone came to Marshall Keeble, the great black gospel preacher, and, pointing to his heart, said, "Brother Keeble, I like to feel it. I like to feel it right here." Brother Keeble had the marvelous ability to respond in an unforgettable way when he was placed on the spot. Pointing to his Bible, he responded to this person, "Well, I like to read it. I like to read it right here." Feelings, of course, are important, but we must not let them lead us. Only the Bible, God's Word, should lead us. When our feelings are based upon our sincere reception and obedience of His Word, we will have the genuine joy spoken of in the New Testament.

How grateful we ought to be that God has given a safe and sure guide for salvation, His Word of truth! In this world of religious confusion, we can turn to the Word and read about the church that God has set up and how one enters it and lives as a part of it.

CONCLUSION

We close the book *The Sequel to the Greatest Story Ever Told* and begin to think about what we have read. It dawns upon us that we have thought about something that is far more significant than anything that appears in our newspapers or on the local or national news on television. We have literally been able to pull back the curtains which conceal the past and, through the inspired Book of Acts, see the most historic and far-reaching event, next to the life, death, and resurrection of Jesus, in the history of the world. We have witnessed the actual beginning of the church, the long-awaited coming of the kingdom of God. With its beginning, we have watched the ushering in of the final age of human history, the Christian Age or "the last days" age.

Another book follows in importance this book that we have read. We could call it *The Third Greatest Story Ever Told* or *The Sequel to the Sequel of the Greatest Story Ever Told*. It would be the story of your conversion to Christ, the story of your becoming a part of the church which Jesus built. The story, of course, would be different for each of us. For many of us the story could easily be written, but for others of us the story could not be written at all because it has not taken place. How is it with you? Has the story taken place? Have you become a New Testament Christian?

If you are not a New Testament Christian, you know now how to become one. By your gladly receiving the Word of the gospel and by your obedience to it, you can be born into the kingdom of God, the very kingdom of heaven we have seen in Acts 2. May our thinking about the next greatest story ever told lead to your making the all-important decision of becoming a Christian.

QUESTIONS FOR STUDY AND DISCUSSION

1. Describe in your own words the reaction of the multitude expressed by the phrase "pierced to the heart."

2. Can you think of a greater tragedy than being in sin?

3. Explain the different emphases that the three accounts of the Great Commission have on the conditions of salvation.
4. Discuss how Acts 22:16 clarifies Acts 2:38.
5. Describe the difficulties which would be present
in an attempt to baptize three thousand people on
one day.
6. What would be the third greatest story ever told?

5

What Christ's Church Looks Like

"So then, those who had received his word were baptized; and there were added that day about three thousand souls" (Acts 2:41).

Photographs are popular with most of us because of their practical and sentimental value. For one thing, they *refresh our memories*. Through the goodness of God, we were part of a type of a preacher's workshop in American Samoa in the summer of 1992. The Samoans are a generous and loving people, and it does not take any visiting brother long to grow to love and appreciate them deeply. They received all who came for the workshop into their hearts the moment we stepped off the plane; consequently, we immediately received them into ours. We took numerous videotapes of the workshop, the church, and our time together. What a treasure they have become! Frequently we watch them and remember our brethren in faraway American Samoa. As certain special scenes appear, we say, "Yes, I remember that moment." Those videotapes bring back to us the faces of the people and all the wonderful times we had with them during that workshop. In a remarkable way, the videotapes stir our memories. Also, pictures aid us as they *clarify the abstract*. As we contemplate an obscure, theoretical thought, a picture can often assist us in eliminating the confusion and lead us to a better understanding of the thought. For example, we might discuss at length the traits of a Christian home without much benefit. If, however, after an explanation of the Christian home is given, we point to an actual Christian home, a home which exemplifies all the qualities of a Christ-centered home, then the concept of the Christian home becomes visible and powerful! The concept has been clarified by the picture. Pictures or models enable us to visualize the reality which is conveyed by the abstract thought.

In His revelation to us, God used both the abstract thought and the picture. He thoroughly explained; then He clearly illustrated. He provided models to go with His mandates, examples to go with His explanations.

We see this particular uniqueness to His revelation in His presentation of the church which Jesus built. He explained in various ways the features and image of Christ's church, and then He gave models or pictures of that church in its actual existence.

The first picture the New Testament gives of the church is found in the latter part of Acts 2. The Gospels have created in us an expectation, an anticipation, for a picture of the church through their record of prophecies about it given by Jesus and His apostles (Matthew 16:18; Mark 9:1; Acts 1:4-8). Then, in Acts 2, as the church is established, a living picture of the church is set before us by the Holy Spirit.

This picture of the church helps us to visualize the dominant characteristics of it. No longer are we left to wonder what the church which Jesus established looks like in real life.

Survey carefully the chief traits of the church in the picture of it given by Luke in Acts 2:

> And they were continually devoting themselves to the apostles' teaching and to fellowship, to the breaking of bread and to prayer.
>
> And everyone kept feeling a sense of awe; and many wonders and signs were taking place through the apostles. And all those who had believed were together, and had all things in common; and they began selling their property and possessions, and were sharing them with all, as anyone might have need. And day by day continuing with one mind in the temple, and breaking bread from house to house, they were taking their meals together with gladness and sincerity of heart, praising God, and having favor with all the people. And the Lord was adding to their number day by day those who were being saved (Acts 2:42-47).

What distinguishing characteristics of the church do we see in this picture?

UNWAVERING IN COMMITMENT

The first trait is a steadfast commitment to the apostles' doctrine or teaching. They were faithfully adhering to God's revelation which had been given to them through the inspired apostles. Luke says, "And they were continually devoting themselves to the apostles' teaching and to fellowship, to the breaking of bread and to prayer" (Acts 2:42).

This commitment of the church to the apostles' teaching manifested itself in a faithful following of their teaching; in their fellowship together in worship, service, and giving; in their observance of the Lord's Supper or the breaking of bread;[1] and in prayer. Christ was their head, and they were recognizing His leadership of His church by honoring His Word which had been given to them through the apostles.

We must not allow the divisions of Christendom to obscure the simplicity of following Christ as His church. The church is not a manmade body. It is a group of people who have yielded to the message of the Holy Spirit and thus, by their obedience to the gospel, have been bonded together by the Holy Spirit into Christ's church. They belong only to Christ. They look to no human leadership but are guided by the head of the body, Christ, through His revealed Word. They view faithfulness to Christ in terms of abiding in His inspired Word.

David Lipscomb sincerely believed that he was living as a member of Christ's church. He was never received into any denomination. He wore only the name "Christian" and sought to follow the Scriptures in every detail. His devotion to Christ was seen in his daily searching of the Scriptures and in his preaching and teaching of them. Living with the Scriptures became so much a part of him that when old age took his eyesight, he would still sit on his porch in the cool of the evening with his Bible on his lap. Even though his

---

[1]The frequency of the observance of the Lord's Supper is not discussed in this passage by Luke, but he does intimate in Acts 20:7 that the supper was partaken by the church every first day of the week, the day on which Jesus arose.

Bible may have been upside down, he had it tenderly placed on his lap. A lifetime of pursuing Christ's will as revealed in the Scriptures was reflected in the comfort he found in his old age by holding the precious Word on his lap even though he could not read it.[2]

The church of Christ can exist only where people obey Christ's gospel and abide daily in His inspired Word. It must be a faithful, continual abiding. Our worship is guided by it, our work as Christ's hands in the world is guided by it, and our daily living for Christ is guided by it.

As we look at the Holy Spirit's picture of the church, the trait of unwavering commitment comes before us.

UNSELFISH IN COMPASSION

Another characteristic that we cannot miss in this divine picture of the church is the church's unselfish compassion for each other. Their sincere obedience to the truth produced in them a compassionate love for each other. Luke says, "And they began selling their property and possessions, and were sharing them with all, as anyone might have need" (Acts 2:45).

Jews had come from all over the Roman Empire to keep the Day of Pentecost. They thought that this Pentecost would be a normal one; but, to their complete surprise, it was not. It was the historic day toward which the prophets had looked. After hearing Peter's message, many of the Jews decided to become Christians (Acts 2:41). Their obedience to Christ meant a radical change for them. For one thing, they needed to stay in Jerusalem and be taught further by the apostles

---

[2]Earl West, *The Life and Times of David Lipscomb* (Henderson, Tenn.: Religious Book Service, 1954), 281.

about the church of which they had become a part. The sudden decision to stay in Jerusalem would be difficult for some of them because they had made no advance plans for such a stay. They would need housing and food, no doubt. How did other Christians who did not face such a crisis respond to these brothers and sisters in distress from distant places? Their response is a picture of compassion and love that is seldom equaled. Some sold houses and land in order to care for these brethren. Their actions illustrate the trait of compassion which Christ intended always to be a part of His church.

True Christians have an active brotherly love which is created by God's love dwelling in their hearts.

A truth which makes their giving and sharing beautiful beyond description is that their giving was totally voluntary. It was not coerced or demanded by the apostles (Acts 5:4). It sprang from hearts of tender compassion and Christlike love. Christ had produced in them a new nature, a life of unselfish sympathy.

Their giving was not just giving or sharing so that all might be equal or have the same amount of goods. It was not communal living; it was caring love. They gave to those in need. They satisfied *needs*, not *greeds*. They knew that *every emergency demands urgency*. As people developed needs, others acted in love to meet those needs—even if it called for sacrificial giving!

Luke later says of the church, "For there was not a needy person among them, for all who were owners of land or houses would sell them and bring the proceeds of the sales, and lay them at the apostles' feet; and they would be distributed to each, as any had need" (Acts 4:34, 35). He also said, "And not one of them claimed that anything belonging to him was his own; but all things were common property to them" (Acts 4:32).

I often tell my students at Harding University as they prepare to travel to their homes during a break or for the summer, "If you have car trouble or any other kind of difficulty as you travel, just remember to call your brethren in the town where you are stranded. They will help you." A love and concern for each family member prevails in Christ's church, transcending material possessions and selfish ambitions.

In American Samoa, I was told that each clan of people would care for a needy member of that clan before any luxuries were considered for any other person in the clan. Needs came first; above all other dreams or desires, needs were met. In a similar way, Christ's church should be known for its compassion for each member.

Compassion is a basic attribute of Christ's church. His church cannot exist where faithful adherence to His Word is not present; neither can His church exist unless compassion abounds as an expression of the very heart of Christ. True Christians have an active brotherly love which is created by God's love dwelling in their hearts. John wrote, "But whoever has the world's goods, and beholds his brother in need and closes his heart against him, how does the love of God abide in him?" (1 John 3:17).

In the Spirit's first picture of the church, unselfish compassion is plainly a significant trait.

UNITED IN CHRIST

A third characteristic of Christ's church seen in this picture is its unity. The Holy Spirit, through the obedience of these people to the gospel and their daily adherence to the apostles' teaching, had given the members of Christ's church a oneness of mind. Luke says, "And all those who had believed were together, and had all things in common" (Acts 2:44). He further says, "And day by day continuing with one mind in the temple, and breaking bread from house to house, they were taking their meals together with gladness and sincerity of heart" (Acts 2:46).

As we behold this beautiful unity which existed in the church that Jesus built, let us remind ourselves of the significance of this first picture of the church. This picture gives us the result, the fruition, of Christ's earthly life and death. What kind of church did Christ come to establish or create? Is it an organizational monstrosity with multiple bodies which wear different names, live by different creeds, and have no fellowship with each other? Or did He create a united body over which He reigns as head? On this Day of Pentecost, we see the clearest image in perhaps all of the New Testament of what Christ wants His church to be and of how He wants it to live in the world. This picture unmistakably reveals that unity, a oneness of mind and life, characterized that church. This has to be what Christ desires for His church today. The division which prevails throughout the religious world is a sure sign that man, in his worldly wisdom, has left Christ's church and has manufactured churches of his own.

The unity of the Lord's church can be illustrated in marriage. Two people who are different in background experiences, family life, and in gender become one in marriage (Ephesians 5:31). After their wedding ceremony, they emerge as a new family. They belong to each other now, and they take on a new nature. Selfish ambitions and personal goals die; new ambitions and goals for the good of this new family come to life. They dwell together in unity, being of one heart and soul, working together for the maintenance, love, and future of their home. How were they given this unity? It was given by their common consent to enter marriage and their fulfillment of the marriage law. How do they maintain this unity? They maintain it by loving each other, caring for each other, forgiving one another, honoring their marriage vows, and honoring the blessed estate of marriage.

On this Day of Pentecost, we see
the clearest image
in perhaps all of the New Testament
of what Christ wants His church
to be and of how He wants it
to live in the world.

Is this not true of the church? How do we enter the unity of the church? By personal consent, we decide to yield our lives to the gospel of Christ and enter His body, the church. As we enter that body, we are united by the Holy Spirit to Christ and to every member of it. With one heart and soul, we begin to love, serve, and live as His body. How do we maintain this unity? We keep it intact by loving and forgiving each other and by honoring the sacred Word of Christ in worship, service, and daily living.

An undeniable characteristic of Christ's church is unity. Christ's true church cannot exist where division remains. We are given this unity by the Holy Spirit when we enter Christ's body; and, as we live as His body, we will either maintain it or mar it. Division in the body of Christ should be unthinkable to every Christian. According to the Holy Spirit's picture, the one place where unity is to be found in this world is in the body of Christ.

CONCLUSION

The Holy Spirit's picture of the New Testament church reveals three striking attributes which set Christ's church apart from all other religious bodies for all time. First, His church is a group of people who have been obedient to His Word and who steadfastly abide in His inspired Word. Second, His church is characterized by compassion for each member, a loving concern which considers a needy member of the church of greater significance than even material concerns and treasures. Third, each person who enters Christ's church through the gospel is made one with Christ and with all the other members by the Holy Spirit and maintains that unity by his love and daily adherence to Christ's Word. The church is pictured as one family with one heart and life!

How, then, can we be Christ's church today? Two words suggest the method: "duplicate" and "dedicate." Let us duplicate the way of becoming a follower of Christ that is found in this chapter. These people heard Christ's Word as it was preached by Peter and cried, "What shall we do?" Peter told them, "Repent, and let each of you be baptized in the name of Jesus Christ for the forgiveness of your sins; . . ." (Acts 2:38).

Through the faith engendered in them by the Word, they repented and were baptized for the forgiveness of their sins, and the Lord added them to His church. This is Christ's way of making us His own. When we follow this way, Christ will do for us what He did for them. He loves us even as He loved them; He died for us even as He died for them.

Having obeyed Christ's Word, let us dedicate ourselves to living as Christ's church. According to the picture in Acts 2, this should be done by adhering to Christ's Word, living with the heart of Christ, and maintaining the unity which the Holy Spirit has given us in Christ.

Do not allow the divided religious world to confuse and distort the beautiful picture that the Holy Spirit has given us of Christ's church. When anyone comes to His Word without prejudice, he can easily see what the church is and what it looks like in the world.

Now that we know what Christ's church looks like, let us ask ourselves, "Do we look like Christ's church?"

QUESTIONS FOR STUDY
AND DISCUSSION

1. Discuss how pictures have been of benefit to you and your family.
2. Why is Acts 2 the first *living* picture of the New Testament church?
3. Discuss the meaning of the phrase "continually devoting themselves to the apostles' teaching" (Acts 2:42). What does this phrase mean for us today?
4. What is meant by "abiding daily in His inspired Word"?

5. Discuss in practical terms the meaning of Christ's being head of the church.
6. Can the church of Christ actually exist when the Word of Christ is not followed?
7. Describe the nature of the emergency which had developed among the new Christians at Jerusalem.
8. Discuss the characteristics of the giving that took place when houses and land were sold and the money was given for those in need.
9. Why should compassion be a characteristic of Christ's church?
10. Describe the type of unity which the Jerusalem church had.
11. Is the Jerusalem church an example of what Christ wants His church to be?
12. Discuss how the unity of the church is entered and how it is maintained today.
13. How is the church of Christ supposed to look today?

6

Christ's Special Word For His People

"And I also say to you that you are Peter, and upon this rock I will build My church; and the gates of Hades shall not overpower it" (Matthew 16:18).

It was the night before Christ's crucifixion, and the ordeal through which He would have to pass was pressing upon His soul with unbearable weight. He took His eleven apostles and went to the Garden of Gethsemane for prayer. He left eight disciples near the entrance of the garden with the gentle command, "Sit here while I go over there and pray" (Matthew 26:36). Then, with Peter, James, and John at His side, He went farther into the garden. After a short distance, He said to them, "My soul is deeply grieved, to the point of death; remain here and keep watch with Me" (Matthew 26:38). Leaving these three, He advanced to a place of solitude and fell on His face and prayed, "My Father, if it is possible, let this cup pass from Me; yet not as I will, but as Thou wilt" (Matthew 26:39).

In our Lord's prayer, a single word looms large in

importance—to Him and to us. In fact, His entire prayer revolves around it. It is the word "yet." The KJV has "nevertheless." It is no understatement to say that the salvation of the world depended upon the spirit indicated by this word.

Suppose Christ, as the only One in the universe who could save mankind, had not wanted to do it. Suppose He had chosen to put Himself first and sinners second. Suppose He had said, "The suffering is too great a price to pay. It is too much of a sacrifice to make for the few who would be saved." Suppose He had prayed, "Father, remove this cup from Me; for not Thy will, but as I will." The answer is obvious: Had He taken this attitude, this spirit, we would be lost and without any possible hope for salvation.

The whole world can rejoice that He placed compassion for sinners and submission to God over His personal wishes. Because our Savior was willing to utter "yet," we now have a way of salvation. Had He not been willing to utter that word, He would never have gone to the cross. Before His "yes" to the Father's will, there had to be a "yet" regarding His own will.

The pivotal meaning of this word "yet" in our Savior's prayer reminds us of the importance of key words in communication. Some words give such significant insight into vital thoughts and truths that they must be carefully studied. To ignore them almost always results in a misunderstanding.

This type of significance attaches to the word "church" because of its key relation to the entire New Testament message. It is an English translation of a word which appears 114 times in the Greek New Testament. It is probably accurate to say that one cannot hope to understand Christ's way of salvation for the world today without understanding the use of this word in the New Testament.

Let us examine this word from the three viewpoints of it which are expressed in the New Testament. These viewpoints convey the rich background of the word, the use Christ and the inspired writers made of it in connection with the redeemed people of God, and the practical application of the word for today.

ITS SECULAR USE

The word was first of all a common, everyday word without any particular religious connotation.

In its simplest meaning, the word appears to have meant an "assembly" of any kind for any purpose. A sample of this use surfaces in Acts 19 in connection with the riot which occurred in Ephesus. A disturbance regarding Christianity developed among the silversmiths who made images to the Asiatic goddess Artemis. The sale of their images was being affected by Paul's preaching Christ in their city. Consequently, the silversmiths gathered with others of similar trades to discuss what could be done about what was happening to their business and religion (Acts 19:25). Demetrius, a silversmith, gave a rousing speech to them and incited the crowd into a frenzied mob (Acts 19:28). The people rushed into a nearby theater, and confusion prevailed. Luke said of their gathering in the theater: "So then, some were shouting one thing and some another, for the *assembly* was in confusion, and the majority did not know for what cause they had come together" (Acts 19:32; emphasis mine). The word used by Luke for the assembly in this verse is *ekklesia*, the word translated into English with our word "church." At first, the crowd thought that their gathering had something to do with Alexander because he had been placed before them. Alexander motioned to them with his hand to get their attention, as he sought an opportunity to speak to the crowd; but recognizing that he was a Jew, the crowd refused to listen to him and cried out for two hours, "Great is Artemis of the Ephesians!" (Acts 19:34). The town clerk eventually appealed to Demetrius to take lawful action against Paul and his companions if he believed they had broken the law. He further said,

> But if you want anything beyond this, it shall be settled in the lawful *assembly*. For indeed we are in danger of being accused of a riot in connection with today's affair, since there is no real cause for it; and in this connection we shall be unable to account for this disorderly gathering (Acts 19:39, 40; emphasis mine).

Luke then added, "And after saying this he dismissed the *assembly*" (Acts 19:41; emphasis mine).

Three times in this account of a secular meeting, Luke used the Greek word *ekklesia* (Acts 19:32, 39, 41). He used it to mean just an assembly, for the assembly he called an *ekklesia* in verses 32 and 41 is pictured as really "a mob" in verse 30. The assembly or *ekklesia* in the theater was not called together; it just happened in all the confusion and flow of events. Luke also called a lawful assembly where legal matters are settled an *ekklesia* in verse 39.

In light of Luke's usage of the word, it is best to think of the word *ekklesia*, in its secular use, as referring to an assembly of any kind. Sometimes an assembly is convened or summoned together, and sometimes an assembly just happens. Luke called both types of assemblies an *ekklesia*.

Some linguists today believe that the secular use of this word in New Testament days had more the meaning of "just an assembly" than the meaning of "a called-out assembly." Luke's use of this word in Acts 19 would seem to confirm their conclusions.

As I grew up on the farm, I had the chore of gathering in the cows for milking in the morning and in the evening. I would take off through our pasture to find them, and once I had found them, I would hurry them to the barn. I would drive them into a lot, a corral, we had, where they would wait to be milked. Often when I would go looking for the cows, I would find the herd grazing in a group instead of scattered out in the pasture. According to the secular use of the word *ekklesia,* the cows in the corral were an *ekklesia,* for they had been gathered into a type of assembly, and the cows in a group in the pasture were also an *ekklesia,* for they had assembled together on their own.

Luke's use of this word gives us an insight into how this word was used in the secular world before our Lord used it in a religious sense. This background of the word will be a basis on which we can build a better understanding of our Lord's use of the word.

ITS RELIGIOUS USE

The word *ekklesia* had also a religious use in the New Testament.

It is clear from the Old Testament that in the Jewish background to Christianity the concept of an assembly of God's people is present. In the Septuagint, the Greek translation of the Old Testament Scriptures, the "congregation" of Israel, which is *qahal* in Hebrew, was translated into Greek with the word *ekklesia,* especially when the "congregation" consisted of Israel gathered before the Lord for religious purposes (Deuteronomy 18:16; 31:30; 1 Kings 8:65; Acts 7:38).

The word "synagogue" was also used originally to refer to an assembly of people gathered together for a specific purpose. Later, the word was applied to an assembly of Christians who had gathered for worship. James used both Greek words, *sunagoge* and *ekklesia*, in his book, apparently because he had Jewish Christians in mind as the readers of his book. He used *sunagoge* for a congregation of Christians who had gathered for worship (James 2:2), and he used *ekklesia* for the body of believers in a given locality (James 5:14).

Thus, as our Lord chose a word that would designate the people who would be God's unique people through His salvation, He selected the word "church" (Matthew 16:18), which probably meant an "assembly" in its secular use but an "assembly of God's people" in its Old Testament connotation. Our Lord took a secular word and gave it a special religious meaning. In His selection of this word, He drew from its secular and religious backgrounds and added new meanings of His own. The word, in the use Jesus gave it, refers to the universal people of God who have been redeemed by His blood, whether they are assembled or not (Acts 8:3; Ephesians 1:22).

Another idea which is brought out in the New Testament in connection with the word *ekklesia* is the concept of one's being "called out" or "set apart." While this thought was probably not in the secular use of the word, it is an important part of the meaning in Christ's special use of it. This idea is projected into the word by the nature of the people designated.

Peter told the multitude on the Day of Pentecost,

"For the promise is for you and your children, and for all who are far off, as many as the Lord our God shall call to Himself" (Acts 2:39). Paul told the Thessalonians to "walk in a manner worthy of the God who calls you into His own kingdom and glory" (1 Thessalonians 2:12). It was through the gospel that God had called them. Paul said, "And it was for this He called you through our gospel, that you may gain the glory of our Lord Jesus Christ" (2 Thessalonians 2:14). Thus, those people who were called to God through the gospel were called "the church" (1 Corinthians 1:1-3).

Although no Christian today is a member of the congregation which was established on Pentecost, all true Christians of all times and of all places are members of the same church of the Lord which was established on that day.

Furthermore, Paul told the church at Colossae, "For He delivered us from the domain of darkness, and transferred us to the kingdom of His beloved Son, in whom we have redemption, the forgiveness of sins" (Colossians 1:13, 14). Peter said to "proclaim the excellencies of Him who has called you out of darkness into His marvelous light" (1 Peter 2:9). Peter also wrote, "But like the Holy One who called you, be holy yourselves also in all your behavior" (1 Peter 1:15).

Saul of Tarsus, the Pharisee, became Paul, the Christian, through answering the call of God by obeying the gospel. When Christ appeared to him on the road to Damascus, Saul believed in Him, repented of his former way of life, and confessed Christ as Lord. Three days later, at Damascus, Ananias told him, "And now why do you delay? Arise, and be baptized, and wash away your sins, calling on His name" (Acts 22:16). Saul, upon receiving these instructions, arose and called upon His name for salvation by being baptized. Later, Paul referred to his becoming a Christian as his being called through God's grace (Galatians 1:15). Thus, Saul was called, set apart, or made a Christian, and as such, was added by the Lord to the body of redeemed people which Christ called His church.

Jesus used the word "church" to refer to all of God's people in the New Covenant period without respect to locality or particular time. Although no Christian today is a member of the congregation which was established on Pentecost, all true Christians of all times and of all places are members of the same church of the Lord which was established on that day. The church was established once for all time in Jerusalem on the first Pentecost Day after Jesus' resurrection. It had but one birthday; it is not born again and again each century or after periods of apostasy.

ITS PRACTICAL USE

We would expect the meaning given to the word "church" by Jesus and the Holy Spirit to be brought out in a practical way in the New Testament, and this we indeed find to be the case.

In practical use, inspired writers used this word in four ways. First, they used it in *a congregational sense*, regarding a congregation of God's people in a given locality. Paul wrote unto "the church of God" at Corinth, to those who had been sanctified in Christ Jesus (1 Corinthians 1:2). The church in Philippi was referred to as "the saints in Christ Jesus who are in Philippi" (Philippians 1:1). The saints in Thessalonica were referred to as "the church of the Thessalonians in God the Father and the Lord Jesus Christ" (1 Thessalonians 1:1). All the Christians in a given locality were called "the church" of that place. An expression of the universal church is the local congregation of Christians. When one becomes a member of Christ's church, he will be a part of the body of Christians where he lives.

Second, the inspired writers used this word in *a group sense*, concerning the local congregations of a region. Luke wrote, "So the church throughout all Judea and Galilee and Samaria enjoyed peace, being built up; and, going on in the fear of the Lord and in the comfort of the Holy Spirit, it continued to increase" (Acts 9:31). Sometimes the church in a region was designated in the plural as "churches." Paul wrote to "the churches of Galatia" as he wrote his letter Galatians (Galatians 1:2). It would be a scriptural use of the word "church" to speak of the church in Europe or the churches in Europe.

Third, the New Testament writers used the word in *a composition sense*. They used it regarding the type or make-up of the churches. Paul referred to "the Gentile churches" in his greetings of Romans 16: "Greet Prisca and Aquila, my fellow workers in Christ Jesus, who for my life risked their own necks, to whom not only do I give thanks, but also all the churches of the Gentiles; also greet the church that is in their house. . . ." (Romans 16:3-5).

Fourth, these inspired writers used the word "church" in *an assembly sense*, in reference to a congregation gathered for worship. The church exists when it is not assembled for worship, but the word "church" is used in a special way for the assembly of the church in a given locality. Paul said the Corinthians came together as a church when they assembled themselves together (1 Corinthians 11:18). He told women to keep silent in the churches: "Let the women keep silent in the churches; for they are not permitted to speak, but let them subject themselves, just as the Law also says" (1 Corinthians 14:34). He is obviously referring to the worship assembly of the church in this passage.

Whether one refers to the church in a universal sense, a congregational sense, a group sense, a compositional sense, or an assembly sense, he is speaking of those who have been brought into the body of Christ by submission to the gospel of Christ. A Christian has been called out of the world and darkness and placed by God's grace into that body which Christ and the inspired writers of the New Testament called "the church."

CONCLUSION

Are you in this church? Do you see the need to come into Christ's church if you are not in His body?

Do you not see what Christ meant by the word "church"? He took a word, which in its secular sense meant "assembly" and in its Jewish connotation meant "an assembly of the people of God," gave additional meaning to it, and applied it to the people who are called into salvation through the gospel of God's grace. In its broad import, therefore, it refers to all those who have been redeemed by the blood of Christ. In a local, practical sense, however, it refers to those He has saved and who are meeting together for worship.

Someone has said, "The church does not save us,

but it contains the saved." Jesus is the Savior of the world, and the ones He has saved He calls His church.

The one who has been saved by Christ will love all others who have been saved by Him. He will have an affinity for them and will want to be with them that he might be strengthened in his faith by them and that he might in some way strengthen their faith. Through His inspired apostles, Christ has instructed His saved people to meet together in worship and to work together in the fulfillment of His mission (Hebrews 10:25; Titus 3:1). This grouping together of His saved people in a given locality in worship and work is the church of Christ.

Would Christ call you His church?

QUESTIONS FOR STUDY AND DISCUSSION

1. Explain the significance of the word "yet" in our Savior's Gethsemane prayer of Matthew 26:39.
2. How often does the word "church" appear in the New Testament, and what significance does this suggest about the word?
3. Give the simple secular use of the word "church" as reflected in the New Testament. Cite a verse where it is so used.
4. Does the word "church" in its secular sense always refer to a religious assembly? Does it always refer to a "called-out" assembly, one that is called together for a special purpose?
5. Does the Old Testament contain the concept of an assembly of God's people? How is this concept translated into Greek?
6. What was the meaning of the word "synagogue"?

7. How does James use the Greek words *sunagoge* and *ekklesia* in his New Testament book?
8. What new concept was added to the word "church" through the Holy Spirit's use of it? (See Acts 2:39 and 1 Thessalonians 2:12.)
9. How does God call people to Himself today? Cite passages of Scripture which support your answer.
10. Explain how Saul was called of God to be a Christian. (See especially Acts 22:16.)
11. How does God call us into His salvation today?
12. Discuss the practical use of the word "church" as it appears in the New Testament.

7

The King, the Kingdom, And the Church

"From that time Jesus began to preach and say, 'Repent; for the kingdom of heaven is at hand'" *(Matthew 4:17).*

What comes to your mind when you try to visualize what heaven is going to be like? Do you envision walking down streets of gold in continual fellowship with all the redeemed? Do you think of worshiping in front of the throne of God in a vast, innumerable throng, giving praise to God and doing His bidding forever?

We can safely make two affirmations about our human view of heaven: First, heaven will be different from our expectations. God has used symbols and figures in the Bible to convey to us what heaven will be like, describing heaven in accommodative terms of what we can understand, not in terms of what heaven actually is. The reality of heaven will be similar to, though different from, the symbols used to describe it.

If you were trying to describe an airplane to someone who had never seen one or heard about one, what would you say? Most likely you would say, "It is like a bird, but it carries people inside it." Your description would be accurate, although a plane is much different from the figure you used. When the person actually saw a plane and rode in one, he would say, "A plane is different from the way you described it!" Surely this is true of our picture of heaven. Even though our picture is based upon the figurative representation given in the Scriptures, we will find that heaven will be different from what we have envisioned.

Second, heaven will be greater than our expectations. The reality is not only different from but also greater than the symbols used to picture it. Heaven will not have literal streets of gold; it will be even more beautiful than gold and other precious metals. Heaven's beauty will transcend the most beautiful things we see and know in this life.

When we experience the reality of heaven, we will say, "Heaven is different from what I expected. It is far greater than any anticipation I had concerning it even though I had inspired figures and symbols in the Scriptures to assist me in picturing it."

This truth regarding heaven illustrates the development of another subject which appears often in the Scriptures. The kingdom of God is both foretold and revealed, anticipated and realized, within the two testaments of the Bible. It was prophesied in the Old Testament and in the early part of the New Testament, and it is presented as a reality on earth in Acts 2 and throughout the remainder of the New Testament. Therefore, we are able to see how it was pictured in prophecy and how it looked when it actually came. Since the kingdom was sometimes portrayed in figures and symbols in prophecy, the reality of it is greater and more glorious than the picture of it given by the prophets. The prophetic picture was accurate, but it was veiled in mystery because of the figurative language which was used.

The word "kingdom" is a significant word in the New Testament as well as in the Old, but we are especially interested in its use in the New Testament because in its New Testament use we see the fulfillment of the Old Testament prophecies. One is at a loss to understand the church of the New Testament without a thorough grasp of the use of this word in the Bible.

Let us examine this word from three angles, each of which relates to its use in conjunction with the church which Christ established.

ITS POLITICAL USE

The word "kingdom" is first used in the Bible in a political sense, in reference to one who is the supreme head, the sovereign, the potentate of a realm.

A king is a ruler, and a kingdom is the domain over which the ruler reigns. The first reference to a "kingdom" in the Bible is in connection with Nimrod, and it serves to illustrate what a king and kingdom are. Genesis relates:

> Now Cush became the father of Nimrod; he became a mighty one on the earth. He was a mighty hunter before the Lord; therefore it is said, "Like Nimrod a mighty hunter before the Lord." And the beginning of his kingdom was Babel and Erech and Accad and Calneh, in the land of Shinar (Genesis 10:8-10).

Nimrod established a domain over which he ruled as king.

The extent of the dominion of some kings in Bible times was limited. Some were even limited to a city. Adoni-bezek, who was captured by Judah and Simeon, claimed that seventy former kings had eaten scraps under his table (Judges 1:4-7). Other kings became absolute monarchs over vast domains and exercised their power with almost unlimited control over the subjects of their empires. Ahasuerus, the king of the Persian world empire, could authorize the writing of a law that would command the massacre of the Jews living within his empire (Esther 3:10-15). He was the sovereign of Persia, with absolute power.

More than one-third of Jesus'
parables unfold truths
about the kingdom.

The political use of the word "kingdom" is also illustrated by Jehovah's relationship with the nation of Israel. At first in Israel's history, God is their king. He is the Sovereign Head of their government as well as the Head of their religion. Israel's government at this time was a *theocracy*, a nation ruled by God. Moses and the sons of Israel, when they saw that God had destroyed the Egyptians in the Red Sea, sang, "The Lord shall reign forever and ever" (Exodus 15:18). As Israel encamped in front of Mount Sinai, the nation was told by the Lord, "Now then, if you will indeed obey My voice and keep My covenant, then you shall be My own possession among all the peoples, for all the earth is Mine; and you shall be to Me a kingdom of priests and a holy nation" (Exodus 19:5, 6). Jehovah gave Israel the laws by which they were to live, and all justice and religious activities were administered in His name. He led Israel in her battles and received credit for her victories (Numbers 21:34). He was the King of Israel, and Israel, as a nation under His rule, was His domain.

During the days of Samuel, Israel, motivated by the desire to be like the nations around her, asked that God give her an earthly king. God granted the people's request and gave them Saul as their first king. The king of Israel was not to be a monarch in the strictest use of the term. He was responsible to Jehovah as a vice regent and servant. His authority was to be limited by the law of Moses. He was to be the servant of Jehovah and was to serve as His earthly representative. He was to defend Israel against enemies, lead Israel in righteousness, and bind the nation together in unity.

A kingdom in the political sense, then, involved a king who was sovereign, a domain of some kind, subjects over which to rule, and laws emanating from the king with which his rule was carried out. Kingdoms could be large or small; they could involve a domain of physical land or a nomadic nation. The dominant idea in the word "kingdom" is the rule of a king and the submission of a citizenry to that king.

ITS PROPHETIC USE

The word "kingdom" also has a prophetic use in the Scriptures. This political term was used by the Holy Spirit to foretell the work which God purposed to do in the world in the last age of the world, the Christian Age.

A major Old Testament "kingdom" prophecy is found in Daniel 2. Daniel was guided by the Holy

Spirit to write, "And in the days of those kings the God of heaven will set up a kingdom which will never be destroyed, and that kingdom will not be left for another people; it will crush and put an end to all these kingdoms, but it will itself endure forever" (Daniel 2:44). Daniel's revelation reveals significant truths regarding the kingdom being prophesied. First, it would be a special kingdom, or a kingly rule, set up by the God of heaven. Second, it would be a kingdom which would be eternal or unending. Third, it would transcend all the other kingdoms of the world in power and endurance.

Moreover, prophecy concerning the coming of this kingdom of God had a place of central importance in the preaching of John the Baptist (Matthew 3:1, 2) and in the preaching and teaching of Jesus (Matthew 4:17). The gospel was spoken of by Christ as the gospel of the kingdom (Matthew 9:35). The twelve and the seventy were sent out by Jesus to announce that the kingdom of heaven was at hand (Matthew 10:7; Luke 10:9). More than one-third of Jesus' parables unfold truths about the kingdom. Jesus taught His disciples to pray for the kingdom to come (Matthew 6:10).

From this emphasis given to the subject of the kingdom in the ministry of John and Christ, several conclusions can be drawn: First, the coming of the kingdom was of great significance in God's plan. Second, the coming of the kingdom was near, "breaking in," or "at hand." Third, the kingdom which was coming was manifestly the fulfillment of Daniel's prophecy. Fourth, the arrival of the kingdom was God's work, not man's. Fifth, when it arrived, the kingdom could only be entered by man when God's conditions of entrance were met (John 3:5).

As one moves through the New Testament, he notices a decreasing use of the word "kingdom," whether it is "the kingdom of heaven," "the kingdom of God," or another phrase referring to the kingdom. References to the kingdom occur forty-nine times in Matthew, fifteen times in Mark, thirty-nine times in Luke, five times in John, eight times in Acts, fourteen times in Paul's Epistles, two times in the General Epistles, two times in Hebrews, and three times in Revelation. Hence, the word "kingdom" has a continued but decreasing use in the New Testament.

The dominant idea in the word "kingdom" is the rule of a king and the submission of a citizenry to that king.

Matthew is the only New Testament writer who uses "kingdom of heaven." Mark, Luke, and John only use "kingdom of God." While the use of the word "kingdom" decreases when one gets to Acts, the use of the term "church" increases. It is as if the term "kingdom" is replaced by the Holy Spirit with the word "church."

From Acts 2 forward, the kingdom is always spoken of as a reality, as being present. Jesus had said to Nicodemus, "Truly, truly, I say to you, unless one is born of water and the Spirit, he cannot enter into the kingdom of God" (John 3:5). But of Philip's preaching Christ in Samaria, Luke writes, "But when they believed Philip preaching the good news about the kingdom of God and the name of Jesus Christ, they were being baptized, men and women alike" (Acts 8:12).

Philip could not have preached this message had the kingdom not been present.

The prophetic use of the word "kingdom," then, refers to the spiritual reign of God over those who have submitted to His will for the world. It refers to a reign and a realm—the reign being the spiritual reign of God over a life, and the realm being the spiritual sphere where that reign of God is evident. This kingly rule of Christ is included in the word "church": As one submits to the will of Christ by receiving the gospel, he is brought into the body of Christ, the church; and as he lives in submission to the head of the church, Christ Jesus, he lives in and as God's earthly kingdom. The kingly rule of Christ over people's hearts creates the church. Thus, "the kingdom of God" and "the church of Christ" are expressions which can be interchanged, as Jesus reveals in Matthew 16:18, 19.

ITS PRESENT-DAY USE

The political background, the prophetic use, and the New Testament reality of the word "kingdom" require a present-day, practical use of the word.

First, it should be used in the sense of *prophetic fulfillment*. The kingdom of which Daniel spoke has come. God's special work in the world in a form of kingly rule, a reign which involves a spiritual realm, is now present. Those who have bowed to the will of God have come under that kingly rule. The prophetic utterances concerning God's coming kingdom have been fulfilled.

Second, we should use the word "kingdom" in the sense of *a present-day reality*. The kingdom of God is no longer something which is to come. Christ reigns now over those who have come into His church through obedient faith. In a sense, our prayer should no longer be, "Your kingdom come," but, "May I fully submit to Your will that You may reign over my life and that I might live in Your kingdom."

— Third, we should use this word in reference to *an earthly expression of God's heavenly rule*. God's specially chosen people, the church, are the earthly expression of His kingdom. Jesus and the New Testament writers have indicated that the church is the realization of the kingdom of God or the kingdom of Christ. Submission to a king creates a citizenship, a kingdom. Jesus called this community of submissive believers His church (Matthew 16:18, 19).

— Fourth, we should see this word in the context of *a spiritual rule*. Faithful Christians are under the spiritual rule of Christ today and anticipate entrance into a fuller and more intimate relationship with God, Christ, and the Holy Spirit in eternity to come. We are the kingdom now, but we anticipate the eternal kingdom which is to come. The word "kingdom" has a future dimension to it. Christ said,

> Not everyone who says to Me, "Lord, Lord," will enter the kingdom of heaven; but he who does the will of My Father who is in heaven. Many will say to Me on that day, "Lord, Lord, did we not prophesy in Your name, and in Your name cast out demons, and in Your name perform many miracles?" And then I will declare to them, "I never knew you; depart from Me, you who practice lawlessness" (Matthew 7:21-23).

Paul wrote, "The Lord will deliver me from every evil deed, and will bring me safely to His heavenly kingdom; to Him be the glory forever and ever. Amen"

(2 Timothy 4:18). Paul was in the kingdom of God, but he anticipated entrance into the heavenly kingdom. He saw the kingdom as a fulfillment of Old and New Testament prophecy, both as a present-day reality expressed in the church which Christ built and an anticipation for eternity.

CONCLUSION

Surely this cursory study of the word "kingdom" teaches us that the challenge of God is to enter His kingdom and live under His divine rule.

As one studies the prophecy of Daniel and the prophecies of John and Christ, he wonders what the kingdom which they were predicting was going to be like. Some of the people of Christ's day had a difficult time eliminating from their thinking a physical-kingdom concept. They looked for a king who would lead them out from under their oppressors. They saw the kingdom in terms of power, might, deliverance, and peace.

When the kingdom came, what God meant by His prophecies becomes clear. Those first people who entered the kingdom probably did not see the kingdom as being exactly like what they were expecting, but what they found as they entered the kingdom was a reign of God expressed in the church in a far greater and more beautiful way than they had anticipated.

The kingdom of God is God's work in the world. Through the long years of the Patriarchal and the Mosaical Ages, He planned and prepared for its coming. He has fulfilled all that He inspired His prophets to foretell, and His kingdom is now here.

The crucial question for us is this: Have we become God's kingdom?

QUESTIONS FOR STUDY
AND DISCUSSION

1. Discuss the differences between a symbol or figurative expression and the reality. Are they the same, or is the reality greater than the symbol?
2. Should we expect the fulfillment of a prophecy which contains symbols and figures to be greater than the symbols and figures of the prophecy?
3. Give a basic definition of a political kingdom.
4. Describe the first kingdom mentioned in the Bible.
5. Describe the differences between the kingdoms of Adoni-bezek and Ahasuerus.
6. Discuss God's relationship to Israel in terms of a king and kingdom.
7. What responsibilities did Saul, the first king of Israel, have as the king over God's kingdom, Israel?
8. What implications can be drawn from Daniel's prophecy concerning the coming kingdom? (See Daniel 2:44.)
9. What implications can be drawn from John the Baptist's and Jesus' prophecies concerning the kingdom?
10. Notice the decreasing use of the word "kingdom" in the New Testament. What implication does this fact suggest?
11. How is one brought into the kingdom of God today, according to the New Testament?
12. Discuss the present-day use of the word "kingdom" which is demanded by the political and prophetic backgrounds to the word.
13. Explain how one can be in the kingdom of God today and yet anticipate the eternal kingdom. (See 2 Timothy 4:18.)

8

The Divine Designations Of the Church, 1

"He is also head of the body, the church; and He is the beginning, the first-born from the dead; . . ." (Colossians 1:18).

The first Day of Pentecost after the resurrection of Christ was a long-awaited day. Important days come, and really important days come! This Pentecost was a day of supreme and lasting importance. It was the day toward which all the Old Testament and the earthly ministry of Christ had looked. Prophecies which had been uttered through the Holy Spirit long before were fulfilled on this day with the coming of God's kingdom. The earthly ministry of Christ was God's unique preparation for this special day.

Shortly before Christ ascended back to His Father in heaven, He commanded His apostles to wait in Jerusalem for the promise of the Father (Luke 24:46-49). As He spoke to them on their last day together about the coming of the baptism of the Holy Spirit, He said, "Which you heard of from Me; for John baptized with water, but you shall be baptized with the Holy Spirit not many days from now" (Acts 1:4, 5). The time was drawing near, and Christ could say that the Spirit's coming was only days away. Ten days later, the apostles were baptized with the Holy Spirit (Acts 2:1-4). Following this outpouring of the Spirit upon the apostles, the first gospel sermon was preached by the apostle Peter to thousands of Jews who had gathered to see what was happening. Three thousand Jews received God's Word and were baptized into Christ (Acts 2:41). In fulfillment of God's eternal plan, the church was born. Jesus had completed His promise to establish it (Matthew 16:18). The Christian Age, the final age of human history, had started with this establishing of the Lord's church.

The church that Jesus built becomes almost the center of focus throughout the remaining part of the New Testament. Congregations of the Lord's church appear in city after city throughout the Roman Empire. Christianity spreads throughout the world like a raging fire as men and women are added to the kingdom of God through obedience to the Word of the Lord.

This beginning of the church raises the questions "How will this church which Jesus established be designated in the New Testament?" and "How will this church be known?"

A thoughtful reading of the New Testament reveals that the church was created to be a special organism and is, therefore, referred to in a special way by the inspired writers. These designations can be divided into three groups. They are used with marked meaning, expressing function, ownership, and relationship. They were given by divine direction and fulfill a divine purpose.

Consider the divine designations of the church.

DESIGNATIONS OF FUNCTION

Three designations given to the church in the New Testament relate to the function of the church as a body or an organism. These designations highlight what the Lord's church is in purpose, design, and action.

First, what Christ established is referred to simply as "the church" (Colossians 1:18, 24). This phrase means "an assembly of people who have become followers of the Lord." These people are referred to in an assembled sense (1 Corinthians 11:18), a local sense (1 Corinthians 1:2), a regional sense (1 Corinthians 16:1), and a universal sense (Ephesians 5:23). This designation declares the basic meaning of what Christ established—a group of people redeemed by His blood who live for Him, worship Him, and do His work.

Second, the church is referred to as "the body of Christ" (Ephesians 1:22, 23). This designation is some-times used as an illustration of what the church is like in function (1 Corinthians 12:12-27) and sometimes as a term to indicate what the church actually is, as a term of identification. When used as a designation, this phrase stresses the function as well as the relationship of the church: The church is the spiritual body of Christ on earth, and it is related to Christ as a body is to its head. In this spiritual body of Christ, individual Christians are said to function as "members" of the body, each Christian being a member of it and working as part of the body. Paul writes of the church at Corinth, "Now you are Christ's body, and individually members of it" (1 Corinthians 12:27).

Third, the church is referred to as "the kingdom" (Acts 8:12). Sometimes the designation is "the kingdom of heaven" (Matthew 16:18, 19), and sometimes it is "the kingdom of God" (John 3:3). Both phrases reflect the spiritual nature of the dominion and rule of the church/kingdom (John 18:36). The church is a body of followers of Christ who have submitted to the rule of God upon earth. Christ is King and is now reigning over His kingdom, the church (1 Corinthians 15:24, 25). Consequently, the church has a divine head or king, and it is governed by divine authority. Members of the church have bowed to the authority of King Jesus and are living as "citizens" of His spiritual kingdom (Philippians 3:20), though they dwell on earth.

These designations used by the Holy Spirit should not be thought of as mere illustrations. An illustration is an analogy, while a specific designation is a term of identification. The New Testament church is often illustrated in the New Testament: It is like a sheepfold (John 10:1), a vineyard (Matthew 20:1), or a precious pearl (Matthew 13:45, 46). Illustrations illuminate and clarify a thought; they throw light on the subject. These illustrations of the church help us to understand the church better, but they are only illustrations, not designations.

DESIGNATIONS OF OWNERSHIP

Two designations found in the New Testament emphasize the possession-type of relationship that the church sustains to God and Christ. These designations suggest ownership and leadership.

First, the church is referred to as "the church of Christ." In Paul's conclusion to his letter to the Romans, he sent greetings from the churches of Achaia by saying, "All the churches of Christ greet you" (Romans 16:16). This designation emphasizes the church's ownership, the church's identity. The church is the church of Christ because Christ founded it, purchased it, owns it, and serves as its head. When we are converted to Christ, we belong to Christ (1 Corinthians 6:20). We become so completely identified with Christ that we are called Christians, followers of Christ (Acts 11:26; 26:28; 1 Peter 4:16). This special assembly of followers of Christ, then, is called the church of Christ to indicate possession, identity, and fellowship.

Second, the church is referred to as "the church of God" (1 Corinthians 1:2). If the church is designated in the New Testament as the church of Christ, we would also expect it to be referred to as the church of God, for Jesus said that He and His Father are one (John 10:30). God planned the church before the foundation of the world (Ephesians 3:10, 11). He sent Christ into the world to prepare for the church (Matthew 16:18) and to purchase it with His blood (Acts 20:28). Just as God was in Christ at the cross reconciling the world to Himself (2 Corinthians 5:19), even so God was with Christ in the founding and purchasing of the church.

One of the important purposes of designations is to indicate identity. The worst experience I had in grade school came in the sixth grade. I had attended grades one through five in a country two-room school building. During the sixth grade, I was moved to a big city grade school, a school with many rooms and many teachers. It was a big change for me. My teacher was a very good teacher, but she accidentally got my name wrong when I first came. For what seemed to me to be the next six months, she called me by the wrong name. I was frustrated and confused. I felt as though I were another person. At times I felt like saying, "Let me be me! Call me by my real name. I am Eddie, not Charles!"

The New Testament church has proper designations, and they should be used. We confuse the identity of the church by using nonbiblical designations for the church. If a group of people seek to be the New Testament church and want to be known as the New Testament church, they should use the designations in the New Testament for the church. A church can call itself the New Testament church and not be the New Testament church; but if it truly is the New Testament church, it should refer to itself with the proper New Testament language.

DESIGNATIONS OF RELATIONSHIP
Two designations in the New Testament stress the idea of relationship. This is expected, since being a member of the Lord's church involves various relationships.

First, the New Testament describes the church as "the family of God." Paul said we are "of God's household" (Ephesians 2:19). He told Timothy that he was writing to him so that he might know how to conduct himself in "the household of God, which is the church of the living God" (1 Timothy 3:15). At our conversion to Christ, God adopted us as His children, giving us family privileges and making us heirs with Christ of eternal life (Romans 8:15-17; Ephesians 1:5). So then, as Christians, we have a heavenly Father to pray to and a loving Savior, our elder brother, Jesus, to pray through. We have brothers and sisters to love and look to for encouragement and support (Acts 2:44). The early church, therefore, looked at each other as brethren and friends (2 Peter 3:15; 3 John 14[1]).

---

[1] The Greek text splits 3 John 14 into two verses, creating verse 15.

Second, the first-century church was referred to as "the disciples of the Lord" (Acts 9:1). The word "disciple" means learner or follower. Christ had commanded His apostles to go and make disciples in His Great Commission: "Go therefore and make disciples of all the nations, . . ." (Matthew 28:19). Christians are disciples of Christ. Sometimes the church is simply referred to as "the disciples" (Acts 9:26; 11:26).

*If a group of people seek to be
the New Testament church
and want to be known as
the New Testament church,
they should use the designations
in the New Testament
for the church.*

The word "disciple" suggests the continual relationship which exists between the Christian and his Lord. The disciple is ever learning from his Lord by imitation and instruction. His Lord is his Master (John 13:13), and he is his Lord's servant (Philippians 1:1).

Third, the New Testament church is called "the temple of God." Paul said to the Christians at Corinth, "Do you not know that you are a temple of God, and that the Spirit of God dwells in you?" (1 Corinthians 3:16). The church as an assembly of Christians forms a dwelling place for God. God's sanctuary today is a living body, the church. Individual Christians are thus called "saints" because they are set apart by the gospel to do sacred work and to provide a dwelling place for God (1 Corinthians 1:2).

Fourth, the New Testament in one passage refers to the church as "the church of the first-born" (Hebrews

12:23). The church sustains a unique relationship with the future because each member of the church is "enrolled in heaven." The future for the Christian does not hold fear and forebodings because of the eternal hope Christ gives Him.

These relationship-type designations give insight into what the church is and how the church should live. They tell us about our life here and our future.

God changed Abram's name to Abraham because the name Abram no longer fit him. Abram was told that he would be the father of a multitude (Genesis 17:5). The name Abram means "exalted father." Abram was a meaningful name, but it would not represent the future Abram would have. The name Abraham means "father of a multitude," a name that would be appropriate for a man who would father a nation of people. The designation God gave Abraham meant something to God and to Abraham. Even so, these designations God gave the church mean something to God, and they should mean much to us.

CONCLUSION

"Why would God care about how the church is designated?" someone may ask. Is not the answer obvious? These designations identify, characterize, and describe the church. God's planning from eternity past, the earthly ministry of Jesus, and Jesus' sacrificial gift on Calvary are all fulfilled in the establishment of the church. How precious the church must be to God! Do we dare designate His church in other ways than the ways He chose?

Assuredly, then, our commitment to being God's church today must be reflected even in the way we designate and describe ourselves. Calling ourselves what God called His church will be at least a beginning place of bringing into reality, into living and practice, God's design and function for the church. When we call ourselves what God called the church, we set ourselves on the right track of what we are trying to be and become.

QUESTIONS FOR STUDY AND DISCUSSION

1. Recount the events which led to the establishment of the church.
2. List the designations of function for the church.
3. What is the basic meaning of the word "church"?
4. Briefly discuss the meaning of the word "body" as a designation of the church.
5. How is the word "kingdom" used in the New Testament in connection with the church?
6. List the designations of ownership for the Lord's church.
7. Why does Paul refer to the church as "the church of Christ"?
8. Why is the church also referred to in the New Testament as "the church of God"?
9. Why should we use the designations for the church that are given in the New Testament?
10. List the designations of the church which stress its relationships.
11. Why is the church called "the family of God"?
12. What is the basic meaning of the word "disciple"?
13. In what way is the church "the temple of God"?
14. Is there really significance in designations?
15. What is accomplished when we refer to the church the way the Bible does?

9

The Divine Designations Of the Church, 2

". . . for an entire year they met with the church, and taught considerable numbers; and the disciples were first called Christians in Antioch" (Acts 11:26).

We often use the expression "It depends on how you look at it." This popular saying reminds us that subjects should be considered from different points of view.

One really does not have in mind the total picture of a subject until he unites into one picture all the different aspects of that subject. For example, one can look at a college education from different viewpoints. Some see it as a necessary step to being successful in the world of business, others see it as an opportunity to improve one's life, and still others see it as a social experience. Most of us believe that the best approach to a college education takes in, to some degree, all three perspectives. In other words, it is not until one brings all these separate facets of a college education into one picture that he has an accurate picture of what takes place during a college career.

Some facts concerning a subject may be missed entirely unless the subject is studied from several points of view. The church is no exception. We should study it from all viewpoints to get the total picture. The church is like a diamond. Any angle of view will reflect the beauty of its multicolored radiance.

That God intended for us to look at the church from various perspectives is indicated by His numerous ways of referring to the church and His people. One cannot see the true nature of the church without considering all of its distinct features.

The designations the Holy Spirit used for God's people assist us in looking at the nature of the church. Each divine designation expresses a characteristic that should be true of members of Christ's church. When we bring these traits together, we can see more clearly what God intended His church to be.

AS CHRISTIANS

First, the New Testament designates members of Christ's church as "Christians." Inasmuch as we are followers of Christ, we are Christians.

The name Christian was first given to the disciples at Antioch: ". . . And it came about that for an entire year they met with the church, and taught considerable numbers; and the disciples were first called Christians in Antioch" (Acts 11:26). The circumstances of the giving of this name are unclear, but we can be certain that God chose it for His people. As a designation, it is found three times in the New Testament (Acts 11:26; 26:28; 1 Peter 4:16). The word highlights our relationship with Christ. We are followers of Him, and therefore, we wear His name.

Paul described his religious life after becoming a Christian in the now famous words, "For to me, to live is Christ, and to die is gain" (Philippians 1:21). Christ was not just first in Paul's life—Christ was his life! The sum and substance of Paul's life was Christ. He was truly a Christian.

AS CHILDREN OF GOD

Second, the members of the church are referred to as "the children of God." In our relationship with God, we are God's children.

At conversion, we were adopted as God's children (Ephesians 1:5). God sent His Holy Spirit into our hearts, and He cries, "Abba, Father" (Galatians 4:6). As His children, we have an eternal inheritance (Ephesians 1:11) and the strength and support of His earthly family (1 Timothy 3:15; Ephesians 2:19-22). In this spiritual, heavenly family, God is our Father (Matthew 6:9), Jesus is our elder brother (Romans 8:17), and all Christians are our brothers and sisters (2 Peter 3:15; 1 John 2:8-11).

Since we are God's children, God has a special love for us (1 John 3:1). He protects us from the Evil One and provides for our daily needs. Jesus taught that if an earthly father gives nice gifts to his children, how much more can we expect Almighty God, our perfect Father in heaven, to give beautiful gifts to His children when they ask Him (Matthew 7:11)!

AS DISCIPLES

Third, the New Testament refers to the church as "disciples" (Acts 11:26). When we consider our commitment to following Christ, we see ourselves as disciples.

A disciple is one who has committed himself to someone greater than he, one who claims to have learned from the greater one, and one who continuously seeks to learn more from the greater one. He is not just a listener; he is a learner, an understudy.

The word "disciple" is especially used in the Gospels, appearing 238 times in them. It is found twenty-eight times in Acts, and it does not appear at all in the Epistles or Revelation. Perhaps the reason for the obvious change in terminology as we go from the Gospels to Acts to the Epistles is that during Christ's life on earth, His followers were called "disciples" in reference to Him. Afterwards, in Acts, the Epistles, and Revelation, they were called "saints" in reference to their holy calling or "brethren" in relation to one another.

> *The church is Christians, children of God, disciples, servants, citizens, friends, and saints.*

Christ told His apostles before His ascension, "Go therefore and make disciples of all the nations, baptizing them in the name of the Father and the Son and the Holy Spirit, teaching them to observe all that I commanded you; and lo, I am with you always, even to the end of the age" (Matthew 28:19, 20). In this way, He gave a continuing use to the word "disciple," even though it is not often seen in the latter part of the New Testament.

A disciple is a doer of the Word. James said, "But prove yourselves doers of the word, and not merely hearers. . . ." (James 1:22). A disciple is more than a student; he is an imitator of Christ, a follower of Christ.

AS SERVANTS

Fourth, the members of the church are described as "servants." When we think of our submission to Christ, we are servants.

When the New Testament was written, the slave/master relationship was intertwined in the society of the Roman Empire. A slave was totally under the control of his master. He had no rights and no real possessions. He did not even own himself. No wonder this term and relationship is used to illustrate our surrender to Christ and our life under His Word. Paul wrote, "If I were still trying to please men, I would not be a bond-servant of Christ" (Galatians 1:10). He further said, "We are destroying speculations and every lofty thing raised up against the knowledge of God, and we are taking every thought captive to the obedience of Christ" (2 Corinthians 10:5).

Someone has said that every heart has a throne and a cross in it. When we put ourselves on the throne, we place Christ on the cross. But when we put Christ on the throne, where He should be, we must place ourselves on the cross. Paul said, "But may it never be that I should boast, except in the cross of our Lord Jesus Christ, through which the world has been crucified to me, and I to the world" (Galatians 6:14). He further said, "From now on let no one cause trouble for me, for I bear on my body the brand-marks of Jesus" (Galatians 6:17).

AS CITIZENS

Fifth, the church is described as "citizens" of the kingdom of heaven (Matthew 16:18, 19). When we think of our part in the kingdom of God, we see that we are citizens.

"For our citizenship is in heaven, from which also we eagerly wait for a Savior, the Lord Jesus Christ," Paul said (Philippians 3:20). He also wrote, "So then you are no longer strangers and aliens, but you are fellow citizens with the saints, and are of God's household, having been built upon the foundation of the apostles and prophets, Christ Jesus Himself being the corner stone" (Ephesians 2:19, 20). Christ is our King (1 Corinthians 15:24, 25), and only those who live under Christ's rule are in His kingdom (Matthew 7:21).

The kingdom in which we are citizens is the eternal kingdom of which Daniel spoke (Daniel 2:44). The writer of Hebrews described it as an "unshakable" kingdom: "Therefore, since we receive a kingdom which cannot be shaken, let us show gratitude, . . ." (Hebrews 12:28). The next time you ask yourself where you will be one thousand years from today, if you are a Christian, you can tell yourself, "I will be in the eternal kingdom!" God's kingdom is not here today and gone tomorrow—it is eternal.

AS FRIENDS

The church is made up of "friends." Christians stand together in a beautiful comradeship. They are the highest type of friends.

John concluded his third epistle by writing, "Peace be to you. The friends greet you. Greet the friends by name" (3 John 14[1]). He called the Christians around

---

[1] The Greek text splits 3 John 14 into two verses, creating verse 15.

him "friends," and he called the Christians who would be receiving the letter "friends." Jesus called His disciples friends, and John is no doubt using this term after Jesus' example. Jesus had said to His disciples,

> Greater love has no one than this, that one lay down his life for his friends. You are My friends, if you do what I command you. No longer do I call you slaves, for the slave does not know what his master is doing; but I have called you friends, for all things that I have heard from My Father I have made known to you (John 15:13-15).

Someone has said, "A friend is someone who stays with you when everyone else leaves." Jesus is this type of friend. When no one else could help us, He laid down His life for us. Christians are to be this type of friend to each other (1 John 3:16). Christians are "friends."

AS SAINTS

Sixth, the church is made up of "saints," those who have been sanctified. Christians are people who have been set apart as God's chosen people.

Paul addressed the Ephesians by saying, "Paul, an apostle of Christ Jesus by the will of God, to *the saints* who are at Ephesus, and who are faithful in Christ Jesus" (Ephesians 1:1; emphasis mine). The KJV has "peculiar people" in Titus 2:14. The NASB renders this phrase "a people for His own possession." The basic meaning of "holy" or "saint" is "set apart for God." God's church is "a people for God's own possession," a holy people, a people set apart for God. Christians have been called with a holy calling (2 Timothy 1:9);

we are to live in holy conduct and godliness (2 Peter 3:11); we seek to appear before Him on the last day "holy and blameless and beyond reproach" (Colossians 1:22).

Some translations of the Bible have "Saint" in the titles of the Gospels of Matthew, Mark, Luke, and John, and have entitled Revelation "The Revelation of St. John the Divine." These titles to these New Testament books came from man, not God. The New Testament labels everyone in Christ as a "saint." The church is even referred to as "the churches of the saints" (1 Corinthians 14:33). We were set apart for God when we became Christians.

CONCLUSION

The members of Christ's church are referred to in the New Testament in various ways. These are beautiful and attractive designations.

Who is "the church"? The inspired answer is a many-sided one: The church is Christians, children of God, disciples, servants, citizens, friends, and saints.

When someone asks, "What is 'the church'?" it is necessary to picture the church from several viewpoints—as a kingdom, as a relationship with Christ, as the family of God, in terms of submission to Christ, and in relationship to God.

If someone asked you, "What is an elephant?" how would you answer? You would most likely give an answer which included different characteristics of the elephant. You would mention his size, trunk, tail, legs, ears, and maybe other traits. Your answer would be inadequate if you only described his trunk. Likewise, we must see the whole picture to understand what God wants the church to be.

To be the true New Testament church today, we

must strive to be all that the New Testament church is. Are we what "the church" is?

QUESTIONS FOR STUDY
AND DISCUSSION

1. Why should a subject be viewed from different viewpoints?
2. What advantage do we gain when we study the church from different viewpoints?
3. What is the basic meaning of the word "Christian"? How does one live when he lives as a Christian?
4. How does Paul describe his life as a Christian in Philippians 1:21?
5. What does it mean to be a "child of God"? Give characteristics of this relationship with God.
6. How often does the word "disciple" appear in the New Testament?
7. Why is there a decreasing use in the New Testament of the word "disciple"? Give the characteristics of a disciple.
8. What does it mean to be a "servant" of Christ? Give an illustration of someone living as a servant of Christ.
9. In what way is a Christian a "citizen" of heaven? Give the characteristics of a citizen of heaven.
10. How enduring is the kingdom of God?
11. How did Christ use the term "friend" concerning His disciples? Give an illustration of a Christian living as a "friend."
12. Give the basic meaning of the word "saint." When do we become "saints"?
13. Should we call one another "saints" today?
14. What are the characteristics of a saint?

10

"The Church's One Foundation"

"For no man can lay a foundation other than the one which is laid, which is Jesus Christ" (1 Corinthians 3:11).

Surely one of the most disheartening realizations to a family is their becoming aware that their house is sitting upon a cracking foundation. The recognition comes to them slowly, over a period of weeks and months. They begin to notice that a door in the house does not close as it should. Soon cracks begin to appear in their bedroom walls and in other walls of the house. These are only seams at first, but with the passing of time they become ugly cracks. The bricks on the outside of their house begin to show jagged breaks as well. A sad time has come. Reality has to be faced. They have a big problem—their house is sitting on a defective foundation.

The reason this news about their house is so discouraging to them is that it is news of an "unfixable" problem. A bad foundation can be repaired to some extent, but it cannot be completely fixed. If you have a bad foundation, you have two options: You either have to live with this problem by patching it up somehow, or you have to move.

This type of house problem reminds us of the critical function of a foundation. Everything in the actual structure of a house rests upon its foundation. If the foundation is faulty, the whole structure is affected. Do not miss the life-lesson in this: In the matter of living as well as in the matter of building, the proper foundation is vital. When you find yourself on the wrong foundation, you cannot fix it—you just have to live on a cracked foundation or move.

The true church has a sure foundation, a bedrock substructure which will never crack or give way; . . .

This truth must be considered in connection with the church. The true church has a sure foundation, a bedrock substructure which will never crack or give way; a false church has a flawed underpinning, a foundation which cannot stand the test of life and eternity.

Think about how the foundation of the church will provide us with both assurance and assistance. An awareness of the solid foundation of the church will bring assurance to those who are members of the New Testament church. They will be reminded that they are part of a body which rests upon a rock which will not crack, crumble, or collapse. Understanding the foundation of the New Testament church will also give a basis for examining the foundations of the false churches in the world; for if the foundation is bad, the whole structure is lacking.

What kind of foundation does the New Testament church, the true church, have? What are its characteristics?

UPON JESUS CHRIST

A characteristic of the foundation of the church which is obvious from reading the Bible is that its foundation is the very deity of Jesus Christ. Its foundation is as strong as the integrity and divine character of Jesus.

Paul used the imagery of building a house as he spoke of establishing a New Testament church. He said, "For no man can lay a foundation other than the one which is laid, *which is Jesus Christ*" (1 Corinthians 3:11; emphasis mine).

Near the end of His earthly ministry, when Jesus and His disciples came near the city of Caesarea Philippi, a strongly fortified city which was situated on a limestone terrace, He asked them, "Who do people say I am?" The current, popular answers were given to Him by the disciples: "Some think You are John the Baptist, some think Elijah, and some think Jeremiah or one of the other prophets." Jesus then asked them the question, "Who do you say that I am?" Simon Peter quickly responded for the whole group of disciples with the reply, "You are the Christ, the anointed One of whom the prophets wrote, and the Son of the living God" (Matthew 16:13-16). Jesus affirmed the correctness of Peter's response by pronouncing a blessing upon Peter: "Blessed are you, Simon Barjona, because flesh and blood did not reveal this to you, but My

Father who is in heaven" (Matthew 16:17). Jesus then stated that upon this rock—the truth which Peter had confessed—He would build His church. "And I also say to you that you are Peter [*petros*], and upon this rock [*petra*] I will build My church; and the gates of Hades shall not overpower it" (Matthew 16:18). The Greek word *petros* means "a stone," but the Greek word *petra* means "a ledge of stone." If our Lord had intended to refer to Peter as the rock upon which He would be building His church, He would have repeated the word *petros*, the word indicating Peter. He used *petra* instead. With this word, He pointed to the truth Peter had uttered about His being the Messiah and the Son of God.

> The Church's one foundation is Jesus Christ her
>   Lord.
> She is His new creation by water and the word.
> From heav'n He came and sought her to be His
>   holy bride.
> With His own blood He bought her.
> And for her life He died.
>
> S. J. Stone

Weigh thoughtfully the firm foundation upon which the church of Christ rests. Its foundation has *integrity*, for it is Jesus' Sonship, a truth which cannot one day be proven false. Think of the fear that would haunt us, the misery that would plague us, if the slightest possibility existed that one day the belief upon which we have structured our lives would be proven fraudulent. Thus, the foundation of the church has *indestructibility*. The attacks of sin, Satan, and the world cannot chip it away. When the sunrise of eternity sends its rays of the never-ending tomorrow across our lives, the foundation of the church will still be as strong as it is today.

UPON THE PROPHETS

Another characteristic of the foundation of the church is that it rests upon the fulfillment of all the divine prophecies which God has given through His Holy Spirit. As Paul pictured the foundation of the family or household of God in Ephesians 2, he said that we have been "built upon the foundation of the apostles *and prophets,* Christ Jesus Himself being the corner stone" (v. 20; emphasis mine).

The prophecies of both the Old and New Testaments converge and find their fulfillment in Jesus and His church, the eternal kingdom. Daniel saw a day when the God of heaven would "set up a kingdom" which would "never be destroyed," a kingdom that would "not be left for another people"; it would "crush and put an end" to all other kingdoms, but would itself "endure forever" (Daniel 2:44).

At the beginning of the New Testament Era, the angel Gabriel announced to Mary:

> And behold, you will conceive in your womb, and bear a son, and you shall name Him Jesus. He will be great, and will be called the Son of the Most High; and the Lord God will give Him the throne of His father David; and He will reign over the house of Jacob forever, and His kingdom will have no end (Luke 1:31-33).

Jesus alluded to the fulfillment of these predictions when He promised, "Upon this rock I will build My church; and the gates of Hades shall not overpower it"

(Matthew 16:18). Peter implied their fulfillment on the Day of Pentecost when he said of David, the prophet,

> And so, because he was a prophet, and knew that God had sworn to him with an oath to seat one of his descendants upon his throne, he looked ahead and spoke of the resurrection of the Christ, that He was neither abandoned to Hades, nor did His flesh suffer decay. This Jesus God raised up again, . . . Therefore let all the house of Israel know for certain that God has made Him both Lord and Christ—this Jesus whom you crucified (Acts 2:30-32, 36).

Because of the fulfillment of the prophecies of the Old and New Testament prophets in Jesus and His church as God's eternal kingdom, we can sing with John, "He has made us to be a kingdom, priests to His God and Father; to Him be the glory and the dominion forever and ever. Amen" (Revelation 1:6).

> How firm a foundation, ye saints of the Lord,
> Is laid for your faith in His excellent word!
> What more can He say than to you He has said,
> You who unto Jesus for refuge have fled?
>
> George Keith

As a little boy, I would often try to run away from my shadow. The shadow was there, but it was not there. It moved with me and depicted my form, but it had no substance. Long ago shadowy prophecies portrayed a coming day of reality for the people of God. God's people were never without the prophetic realization that the Messianic Era was on its way and would soon arrive. They looked with joyful anticipation for the day of the eternal kingdom of God. At

Pentecost, the substance and reality of the prophecies appeared; the eternal kingdom in the earthly form of the church began. The reality of God's plan and work burst upon the world.

UPON THE APOSTLES

A third characteristic of the foundation of the church is the truth revealed by inspired apostles. Paul said the family of God was "built upon the foundation *of the apostles* and prophets, Christ Jesus Himself being the corner stone" (Ephesians 2:20; emphasis mine).

Christ put in place the apostolic part of the foundation of the church by training His apostles for over three years. He promised them that after His departure they would be guided into all truth: "But the Helper, the Holy Spirit, whom the Father will send in My name, He will teach you all things, and bring to your remembrance all that I said to you" (John 14:26). This promise was fulfilled when the Holy Spirit was poured out upon them on the Day of Pentecost in Acts 2, and they were thereby equipped for the mission of transmitting God's revelation to other men. The apostles were God's human instruments for the giving of His truth to the world. The church rests upon the divinely inspired apostles and their revelation of God's Word. The true church of Christ can only exist where the Word of God is honored and obeyed.

> Standing on the promises that cannot fail,
> When the howling storms of doubt and fear
>   assail.
> By the living word of God I shall prevail,
> Standing on the promises of God.
>   R. Kelso Carter

The Christian can rejoice that the New Testament church is built upon the solid rock of God's truth, for the foundation of the Lord stands sure (2 Timothy 2:19). Truth is eternal; error is marked for destruction. The church has an eternal tomorrow with God because it is anchored in unbreakable, everlasting truth. The Christian, as part of Christ's body, the church, believes, hopes, and lives upon the granite rock of God's revelation.

CONCLUSION

The church of the New Testament has an enduring foundation: It rests upon the deity of Christ, the prophets of God, and the apostles of Christ—a foundation that is as strong as Jesus, as eternal as truth, and as real and authentic as God's plan for the world.

Are you a member of Christ's church? Remember: if the church of which you are a member has a cracked foundation, you cannot fix it—you must decide to live on that inadequate foundation or move. If the foundation upon which you are living is cracked, please, for the sake of your life and eternity, move. Enter the church of Christ whose foundation will secure you during the storms of life and will provide safe footing for you before our Father's throne in eternity.

QUESTIONS FOR STUDY
AND DISCUSSION

1. Why is it important for the church to have the proper foundation?
2. What is Paul's affirmation about the foundation of the church in 1 Corinthians 3:11?
3. Explain the meaning of Matthew 16:18. Is Peter or

Jesus' deity the rock upon which Jesus said He would build His church?

4. Discuss the integrity and indestructibility of the foundation of the church.

5. In what way would the prophets be within the foundation of the church?

6. What does the angel Gabriel imply in his statement to Mary? (See Luke 1:31-33.)

7. What does Peter declare regarding Jesus in Acts 2:30-32, 36?

8. In what way are the apostles in the foundation of the church?

9. Are living apostles needed today for the church to be built upon the foundation of the apostles?

10. How did the apostles become part of the foundation of the church?

11. What does Paul mean when he says that the "foundation of the Lord stands sure"?

12. If the foundation of a church is wrong, what can be done about it?

11

Christ, The Head Of the Church

"For the husband is the head of the wife, as Christ also is the head of the church, He Himself being the Savior of the body" (Ephesians 5:23).

An old story has it that a group of boys came running into a country store. They bought a few things and rushed out. Within minutes they topped the hill just beyond the store and went out of sight. A few minutes later, another boy came running into the store, out of breath. He excitedly asked the store clerk, "Have you seen a group of boys come by?" The store clerk said, "Yes. They were here not more than fifteen minutes ago. They were in a big hurry and didn't stay long." The boy said, "Which way did they go? I'm their leader!"

This boy, the group's leader, illustrates the kind of leadership all of us have seen too often—a leadership which is not out front leading but is behind wondering which way the followers went! The trouble with human leadership is its frailty and inadequacy. Human

133

leadership, at some time or other, brings disappointment. People are always going to be people.

Must we also expect inadequate leadership for the church at times? Does the ship of Zion have a Captain who is subject to human weakness and mortal failures? As we journey from earth to the eternal shore of the great forever, must we depend upon a broken compass?

Our fears are allayed by the words of inspiration which assert that the head of the church is none other than Jesus Christ. Paul wrote, "Christ also is the head of the church, He Himself being the Savior of the body" (Ephesians 5:23). Let the phrase "Christ also is the head of the church" enter deeply into your thinking. Recognizing Christ as the head of the church will give assurance to those who are members of Christ's church, for doing so reminds them of the unerring guidance they receive. It will also give an incentive to non-Christians to enter the church, that they might come under the infallible leadership of Christ.

Let us contemplate the reassuring theme of "Christ, the Head of the Church," by considering the ways in which He is the head of the church.

HE IS THE HEAD IN AUTHORITY
First, Christ is the head of the church in authority. He is our Lord, and He leads us by His law.

After His resurrection from the dead and His ascension to heaven, Christ was seated at God's right hand in the heavenly places, "far above all rule and authority and power and dominion, and every name that is named, not only in this age, but also in the one to come" (Ephesians 1:21). God "put all things in subjection under His feet, and gave Him as head over

all things to the church, which is His body, . . ."
(Ephesians 1:22, 23). Paul emphasized this same truth
in Colossians, when he said, "He is also head of the
body, the church; and He is the beginning, the first-
born from the dead; so that He Himself might come to
have first place in everything. For it was the Father's
good pleasure for all the fulness to dwell in Him"
(Colossians 1:18, 19). According to the writer of Hebrews, God will speak to us through His Son during the
last days or the Christian dispensation (Hebrews 1:1, 2).
He has highly exalted Jesus and has bestowed on Him
the name which is above every name, "that at the
name of Jesus every knee should bow, of those who
are in heaven, and on earth, and under the earth, and
that every tongue should confess that Jesus Christ is
Lord, . . ." (Philippians 2:10, 11). The Scriptures assure
us that Christ will reign as head of the church or king of
the kingdom until the end of time, and then, when all
rule, authority, and power are abolished, He will deliver the kingdom to God the Father (1 Corinthians
15:23, 24).

Someone has said, "The best government in the
world is a dictatorship, if the dictator is perfect!" This
statement obviously is true, but it does not give us any
comfort regarding the governments of men, for every
earthly dictatorship is flawed with human imperfec-
tion. This saying does, however, give us encouragement concerning the church. The dictator of the church,
the divine Son of God, is perfect in knowledge, wisdom, love, and grace! Learning, therefore, that we as
Christians are under the dictator, Christ, is not bad
news; it is the highest kind of good news. Would we
want it any other way?

As we live as His church, we live in subjection to

His authority and leadership. Even in a "me-istic age," we cannot demand our own way in Christ's church. We cannot say, "Me first," and acknowledge Jesus as Lord at the same time. Every decision we make is a spiritual decision, guided by our submission to His Lordship. Christians sing, "Have Thine Own Way, Lord," not "I Am Going To Do It My Way."

HE IS THE HEAD IN EXAMPLE

Second, Christ is the head of the church in example. He is our perfect pattern in obedience to God. He leads us by His sinless life.

Peter said that Christ committed no sin, and no deceit was found in His mouth. When He was reviled, He did not revile in return. When suffering, He uttered no threats (1 Peter 2:21-23).

Christ never needed to apologize for a mistake He had made. No need ever arose for Him to retract a misspoken word. His heart never knew a sinful thought. His enemies scrutinized His life but were unable to find a single sin.

The head of the church is perfect in character even as He is perfect in authority. He leads His church with His own life. As His church, we are to heed His commands and imitate His life. John wrote, "The one who says he abides in Him ought himself to walk in the same manner as He walked" (1 John 2:6). Because of the unique leadership Jesus gives to the church, Paul could charge others, "Be imitators of me, just as I also am of Christ" (1 Corinthians 11:1).

From one viewpoint, Christ *became* our perfect Savior. By living a perfect life before God, He became perfectly qualified to be our Savior and could offer to God a sinless life for the atonement for sin. The writer of Hebrews argued, "Although He was a Son, He learned obedience from the things which He suffered. And having been made perfect, He became to all those who obey Him the source of eternal salvation" (Hebrews 5:8, 9).

Nathaniel Hawthorne wrote the story "The Great Stone Face" which reminds us that we become what we behold; we imitate what we admire. A gracious face, chiseled in the side of a mountain, overlooked a valley where a village of oppressed people lived. The community believed that someone with a face similar to the great stone face would one day come as their deliverer. A boy of the village continually meditated upon the stone face with aspiration and desire. In time, through his beholding and admiring the stone face, the youth grew into the likeness of the face, and the community soon recognized him as their deliverer.

The truth that we become what we behold is especially true of the church. Paul said, "But we all, with unveiled face beholding as in a mirror the glory of the Lord, are being transformed into the same image from glory to glory, just as from the Lord, the Spirit" (2 Corinthians 3:18).

The church of Christ looks to His life as a model of how to live. He is our head in example. Not only do we look at Him, but we also look unto Him (Hebrews 12:2) as He ever leads us with His perfect life.

HE IS THE HEAD IN LOVE

Third, Christ is the head of the church in love. He leads and commands us with His compelling love.

The evening before His death, Jesus told His disciples, "A new commandment I give to you, that you love one another, *even as I have loved you*, that you also

love one another. By this all men will know that you are
My disciples, if you have love for one another" (John
13:34, 35; emphasis mine). He further told them, "This
is My commandment, that you love one another, *just as
I have loved you*" (John 15:12; emphasis mine).

This love which Christ has for us and beautifully
demonstrates motivates us in three directions: First, it
constrains us *to love Him.* John said, "We love, because
He first loved us" (1 John 4:19). Second, His love
constrains us *to love each other.* John wrote, "We know
love by this, that He laid down His life for us; and we
ought to lay down our lives for the brethren" (1 John
3:16). Third, His love constrains us *to do His will.*
Christ said, "If you love Me, you will keep My commandments" (John 14:15).

---

*Assuredly, Christ is the head
of the church
in authority, in example,
and in love and service.*

As the angels watched the earthly ministry of Christ,
how they must have watched with awe as He, the day
before His death on the cross, took a basin and a towel,
and in love and humility washed His disciples' feet!
The King of kings knelt before His disciples in loving
service. Christ not only became a man, but He became
a servant of men. He took the form of a man and lived
the life of a bondservant (Philippians 2:7).

John introduces this tremendously important
scene with these words: "Jesus, knowing that the
Father had given all things into His hands, and that
He had come forth from God, and was going back to

God" (John 13:3). In other words, at a time when Christ was especially conscious of His authority, position, and future, He condescended to do the work of a servant in harmony with the life of a servant which He had lived. He did not flaunt His supremacy and strength, His power and position. In love, He used it to teach His disciples the lesson of humility.

As the head of the church, He lovingly serves us with His power and authority! He did not relinquish His position as Lord when He washed the disciples' feet; He used His position as Lord to serve them and to inspire in them the spirit of service. He said to them, "You call Me Teacher and Lord; and you are right, for so I am. If I then, the Lord and the Teacher, washed your feet, you also ought to wash one another's feet. For I gave you an example that you also should do as I did to you" (John 13:13-15).

Jesus has portrayed in the highest possible way what love is and how true love is manifested. He leads His church with His love. As we live in the atmosphere of His love, breathe that atmosphere, and respond to it, we are remade by it into His image. No wonder our brother said, "Beloved, let us love one another, for love is from God; and everyone who loves is born of God and knows God. The one who does not love does not know God, for God is love" (1 John 4:7, 8).

CONCLUSION

Assuredly, Christ is the head of the church in authority, in example, and in love and service. He leads His church through His Lordship, through His perfect life, and through His compelling love.

The head of any organization or body gives the credibility, authenticity, and strength he possesses to the organization or body he leads. This is certainly true of Christ and the church. The Christ, the divine Son of God, gives His spotless perfection, infinite wisdom, matchless integrity, and almighty strength to the church with His headship and leadership.

The church of Christ was founded by Christ, is led by Christ, and wears Christ's name. Whatever Christ possesses, He imparts to His church; whatever future Christ has, the church has. He promises to sustain His church today and to sanctify her for her future, "that He might present to Himself the church in all her glory, having no spot or wrinkle or any such thing; but that she should be holy and blameless" (Ephesians 5:27).

If Christ has created the church, imparted to the church His love and salvation, and has crowned the church with His promise of eternal glory, who would not want to be in His church?

Are you the church led by Christ?

QUESTIONS FOR STUDY
AND DISCUSSION

1. Cite examples of leadership which does not really lead.
2. How is Jesus the head of the church in authority? Give passages of Scripture which teach that Jesus has all authority.
3. How long is Christ to reign as head of the church? (See 1 Corinthians 15:23-25.)
4. Why is it encouraging to know that a Christian is led by Christ?
5. How does Jesus lead the church with His life?
6. How did Jesus become our perfect Savior? (See Hebrews 5:8, 9.)

7. Conversion to Christ is an event in time, but transformation into His image is a process over time. Discuss this process of transformation. (See 2 Corinthians 3:18.)
8. How does Christ lead with His love?
9. How does the love of Christ motivate us?
10. What does Christ's washing of the disciples' feet teach us about daily living for Christ?
11. How do we wash each other's feet today?
12. What does a leader contribute to the body that he leads?

12

Entering
The Church

" . . . And the Lord was adding to their number
day by day those who were being saved" (Acts 2:47).

Some things are very expensive but are not really valuable—like a yacht; some things are inexpensive but very valuable—like sunshine or rain; some things are very expensive and very valuable—the church of Christ falls into this category.

The New Testament leaves little doubt about the incomparable worth of the church. Its value is underscored in at least three ways: First, we see its worth in *its unique origin.* It was planned and purposed in the eternal counsel of heaven (Ephesians 3:10, 11), and it was prepared for through the earthly ministry of Jesus (Matthew 4:17). It was a divine forethought, not a mistaken afterthought. Second, we see its worth in *its unrivaled cost.* We are told by Paul that it was purchased by the blood of Christ (Acts 20:28). The ultimate purpose of the death of Christ was to bring the church into existence. If purchase price indicates value,

143

then the church, having been purchased by Christ's blood, is indisputably the most valuable of all earthly bodies. Third, we see its worth in *the unsurpassed value* that is placed upon it. Christ urged us to seek the kingdom of heaven above all other pursuits. He said, "Again, the kingdom of heaven is like a merchant seeking fine pearls, and upon finding one pearl of great value, he went and sold all that he had, and bought it" (Matthew 13:45, 46). He not only likened the church to a precious pearl, but He likened it to the most precious of all pearls!

This supreme value of the church suggests that ignoring the New Testament church would be the greatest of all mistakes. A millionaire becomes the world's poorest pauper if he does not find and enter the Lord's church. The greatest man outside of the church becomes the least of men.

In light of the unmistakable worth of the church, reason dictates that we sincerely ask, "How is the church entered?" Perhaps no greater question can be considered. Let us devote ourselves to finding the New Testament answer to this question.

THE ANSWER ANNOUNCED

Christ was clear and definite about what He wanted His disciples to do after He returned to heaven from His earthly ministry. Three rather full accounts of His commission are recorded in the New Testament (Matthew 28:18-20; Mark 16:15, 16; Luke 24:46, 47). The significance of these accounts can hardly be overestimated. They give Christ's guidance for His disciples for the entire Christian Age.

Christ first gave a worldwide charge to His disciples, by saying, "Go into all the world and preach the

gospel to all creation" (Mark 16:15). Second, He specified the conditions upon which salvation is to be offered as the gospel is preached. He told His disciples
what to do—"Go," and He told them what to say—
"Preach the gospel." With the words "go" and "gospel" He summarized their future work.

One time, according to Mark, Christ gave the commission and emphasized the condition of belief. He
said, "Go into all the world and preach the gospel to
all creation. He who has believed and has been baptized shall be saved; but he who has disbelieved shall
be condemned" (Mark 16:15, 16). Baptism is clearly
mentioned as a condition in this record of the commission, but the emphasis seems to be upon belief.

According to Luke, Christ gave the commission at
another time and stressed repentance. He said, "Thus
it is written, that the Christ should suffer and rise
again from the dead the third day; and that repentance for[1] forgiveness of sins should be proclaimed in
His name to all the nations, beginning from Jerusalem" (Luke 24:46, 47). Repentance, a turning from sin
to God, was to be a dominant note in the gospel
preaching of the Christian Age.

Matthew pictured Christ as giving the commission
on a mountain in Galilee, where He accented baptism.
He said, "All authority has been given to Me in heaven
and on earth. Go therefore and make disciples of all the
nations, baptizing them in the name of the Father and
the Son and the Holy Spirit, teaching them to observe
all that I commanded you; and lo, I am with you
always, even to the end of the age" (Matthew 28:18-20).

Obviously, then, the three conditions upon which

[1]Some manuscripts read "and" here instead of "for."

salvation is to be extended are belief, repentance, and baptism, each of which was singled out by our Savior and stressed in the three accounts of the Great Commission.

These three conditions are evident and are easily perceived. No one can take seriously Jesus' commission without acknowledging these conditions and recognizing their significance in the Lord's plan. They constitute the terms or conditions of entrance into the Lord's kingdom or church. They are to govern the entire Christian Age.

THE ANSWER AMPLIFIED

The conditions of salvation are not only unmistakably given in the New Testament, but they are also graphically illustrated in the Acts of the Apostles.

For example, the book begins with the thrilling story of the establishment of the church. In Acts 2, a multitude of people who were convicted by Peter's sermon cried out, "What shall we do?" Belief in Jesus had prompted their crying out. Peter, consequently, commanded them to repent and be baptized for the forgiveness of sins (Acts 2:38). Three thousand were baptized that day (Acts 2:41). Accordingly, Acts 2:47 says, "And the Lord was adding to their number day by day those who were being saved." The group to which they were added is later referred to as the church (Acts 5:11). Our Lord, in His final commission, had specified faith, repentance, and baptism as the conditions upon which salvation was to be proclaimed. The people who entered the church on Pentecost complied with these three conditions.

Another example is found in Acts 8. In the latter part of Acts 8, Philip was told by an angel to go south for further preaching (Acts 8:26). At a certain intersection, Philip saw an Ethiopian eunuch traveling down the road in a chariot (Acts 8:27, 28). This man was a very religious man, but he was not yet a Christian. Philip was instructed by the Holy Spirit to go near and join the Ethiopian (Acts 8:29). Running to him, he discovered that the Ethiopian was reading in the book of Isaiah but did not understand what he was reading (Acts 8:31). Philip started with the passage which the Ethiopian had been reading and unfolded to him the story of Christ (Acts 8:35), telling him, no doubt, all about Christ's coming into this world and dying for our sins.

As they traveled along, talking about Christ, they soon approached some water. The Ethiopian asked, "Can I be baptized?" Since the Ethiopian believed, it was entirely appropriate for him to be baptized.[2] They stopped the chariot and waded down into the water, and Philip immersed the Ethiopian (Acts 8:38). Following his baptism, the Ethiopian went on his way rejoicing.

Once again, the terms our Lord laid down for salvation in His final commission were followed. Be-

---

[2]Verse 37 of Acts 8 does not appear in many reliable manuscripts of Acts. This has led to the conclusion that this verse may not be part of the original text of the New Testament. It must be granted, however, that the leading statement posed in this verse by Philip is the most natural thought to raise in this circumstance. The Ethiopian eunuch did not know of Christ or about whom the prophet was writing. Then, after only one conversation about Christ, the eunuch wanted to be baptized. Hence, the statement "If you believe with all your heart, you may" is most appropriate and can never be out of place in the preparations made for baptism. The confession of Christ as God's Son is an affirmation of faith and grows out of the condition of the Great Commission to believe.

lief in Christ became a reality as a result of the preaching done by Philip (Acts 8:35, 36). The Ethiopian was a religious man who was sincerely trying to do the will of God. Repentance, therefore, is evident from his acceptance of the message about Christ which Philip brought him. Baptism is portrayed in this account more clearly than in any other in the Book of Acts. Both Philip and the Ethiopian waded down into the water, and Philip immersed him.

Let us look at it another way: Suppose you live in a kingdom and know the king as a personal friend. One day, while in a conversation with the king, you are told that if you will return later to see him, he will forgive your taxes. You receive this news with joy and resolve to return to see him in one month. Eventually, you return to see the king, anticipating the forgiveness of your taxes. Upon your arrival at the palace, you are told that the king has gone on a trip to another country.

Our Lord, in His final commission, had specified faith, repentance, and baptism as the conditions upon which salvation was to be proclaimed.

You tell the royal gatekeeper that the king told you that your taxes would be forgiven if you returned to see him. The gatekeeper says, "The king has made special arrangements for you." He ushers you into a room which is occupied by twelve administrators. You tell them your story. In response, they say, "When the king was here, he had the power to forgive taxes through just a word, but the king is now gone. He left behind specified terms upon which taxes are to be forgiven. You will now have to abide by these terms. You must first return to your home; second, write a letter to us stating your story; third, list all the members of your family; and fourth, sign the letter in the presence of three witnesses. When these terms are met, your taxes will be forgiven."

Compare this story with what Christ has actually done. When He was here, He would often forgive sins with just a word. For example, He forgave the thief on the cross (Luke 23:43). However, when Christ got ready to leave this earth and return to heaven, He gave us the terms upon which salvation would be imparted to people during the Christian Age. In addition, He indicated that His commission was to be in effect until the end of the world (Matthew 28:20). Now that the King is gone, His terms of forgiveness are in effect.

THE ANSWER APPLIED

These terms of entrance into the church should be applied to each of us. The final commission of Christ has not changed. It is the same today as it was when it was given. The terms of salvation are precisely the same for us as they were for those who heard the first sermon preached by Peter. Christ sets the terms of entrance into the church and does the actual adding to it. Men's arguments and instructions do not alter His last will and testament. The King is gone, and the terms He set down for the Christian Age must be followed.

Where are you in respect to His terms of entrance into His church? Have you believed? The source of faith is the Word of God (Romans 10:17). Man's wisdom, learning, or accomplishments cannot produce faith. Do you believe in God? Do you believe that

Christ is His Son and the Savior of mankind? Have you repented of your sins (Acts 17:30, 31)? Have you turned from sin to the living God? Have you committed your heart to the will of God regardless of what it means and regardless of where it leads?

Have you stated publicly that you believe in Jesus as God's Son and Lord (Romans 10:10)? Have you confessed with your lips that Jesus is Savior and Lord?

Have you been baptized? The baptism of the Great Commission is by immersion (Romans 6:4), into Christ (Romans 6:3; Galatians 3:27), for the forgiveness of sins (Acts 2:38; 22:16), and in the name of the Father, the Son, and the Holy Spirit (Matthew 28:19, 20). Have you been baptized according to the New Testament pattern?

When one today adheres to the terms which Christ laid down in His final commission, is it not reasonable to believe that our faithful Lord and Savior adds him to His church or kingdom? No one can explain away the Lord's terms. We must not permit any substitution for them or any corruption of them. Our commitment to Christ will allow nothing but obedience.

CONCLUSION

Have you entered the New Testament church? Would you like to enter it today?

It is surely the greatest and grandest news for us that the church found in the New Testament can be entered by anyone who will sincerely comply with the Lord's terms of entrance. All nations, all races, and all peoples can enter into His kingdom and be one in Christ (Ephesians 2:14).

Wisdom demands that we start at the beginning, making sure the foundation is true. If you are not confident that you have complied with the Lord's terms of salvation, fulfill those terms completely and immediately. Enter His kingdom, and from now on live as a citizen of His kingdom and of His kingdom alone.

The church of Christ is not really valuable to you unless you enter it.

QUESTIONS FOR STUDY AND DISCUSSION

1. Describe the incomparable worth of the Lord's church.
2. List the three full accounts of the Great Commission.
3. Give the special emphasis of each account of the Great Commission.
4. Apply the conditions of the Great Commission to the story of the conversion of the Jews in Acts 2.
5. Apply the conditions of the Great Commission to the story of the conversion of the Ethiopian in Acts 8.
6. Are the conditions of the Great Commission binding upon us today?
7. Why can we not be saved today as the thief on the cross was saved?
8. How can one become a member of the church today?
9. Do men add the saved to the church?
10. Is there any reason to believe that if one does what was done in the Book of Acts to become a Christian that God will not do for him what He did for those who obeyed His will in the Book of Acts?
11. Is the invitation of Christ extended to all people?

12. How can we be sure that we are in Christ's church?
13. If we do not enter Christ's church, do we really consider it valuable to us?
14. When the Lord's conditions of salvation are corrupted, has great damage been done?

13

The Unity
Of the Church

"Now I exhort you, brethren, by the name of our
Lord Jesus Christ, that you all agree, and there be no
divisions among you, but you be made complete in the
same mind and in the same judgment" (1 Corinthians
1:10).

T. B. Larimore, a gospel preacher whose gentle and
Christlike spirit was recognized by all who knew him,
illustrated the family unity of Christ's church with
Psalm 133:1: "Behold, how good and how pleasant it
is for brothers to dwell together in unity!" Brother
Larimore said that some things are good but not pleasant. A visit to the dentist may be good but not pleasant.
An operation to remove a cancerous growth is life-
saving and thus good, but it is not pleasant for the
patient. Then, brother Larimore said that some things
are pleasant but not good. Candy is pleasant to eat, but
it is not always good for us. Recreation is pleasant and
enjoyable on special occasions, but continual recreation would be dissipation. Brother Larimore observed

that one can find a few things in this world that are both good and pleasant, actually beneficial to us and at the same time enjoyable to experience. He concluded that both of these qualities are found in unity in Christ, in brothers dwelling together in one accord.[1] Who of us would not agree with T. B. Larimore?

> *The unity of the believers had to be the dearest and most important longing in the heart of Jesus, or He would not have prayed for it on the night before His death.*

According to the New Testament, unity in Christ is not only good and pleasant to us; but, even more importantly, it is good and pleasing to God. Just before Jesus was betrayed into the hands of lawless men on the darkest night of the world, He prayed for the unity of those who would believe on Him in the future. He prayed to His Father, "I do not ask in behalf of these alone, but for those also who believe in Me through their word; that they may all be one; even as Thou, Father, art in Me, and I in Thee, that they also may be in Us; that the world may believe that Thou didst send Me" (John 17:20, 21).

If you were scheduled to be executed tomorrow, and you knelt to pray tonight, for what would you pray? Would you pray for trivial, unimportant dreams? Would you not pray for the dearest and most important aspirations in the world to you? Do we not see how

---

[1]T. B. Larimore, "Unity," in *Biographies and Sermons*, ed. F. D. Srygley (n.p., n.d.; reprint, Nashville, Tenn.: Gospel Advocate, 1961), 35-36.

Christ valued unity as we read His prayer for unity the night before He was crucified? The unity of the believers had to be the dearest and most important longing in the heart of Jesus, or He would not have prayed for it on the night before His death.

When Paul wrote to the terribly divided church at Corinth, a church beset by numerous problems and weaknesses, he first gave them a forceful call to unity: "Now I exhort you, brethren, by the name of our Lord Jesus Christ, that you all agree, and there be no divisions among you, but you be made complete in the same mind and in the same judgment" (1 Corinthians 1:10). At the time that Paul wrote to the Corinthians, A.D. 54 to 56, denominations did not exist. The only church that existed was the Lord's church, and Paul, by inspiration, tells God's church at Corinth to dwell together in unity. He not only pleads for this unity, but he pleads for it in the very name of Jesus Christ.

Let us look at the unity of the church in greater detail. The two passages already cited make it obvious that Christ's church is to have a beautiful unity, but what kind of unity is it to have? What are the characteristics of it? A deeper understanding of this unity should provide practical assistance for our Christian living and should enhance our understanding of the church itself.

AN ORGANIC UNITY

First, let us recognize the organic unity of the body of Christ. The New Testament speaks of a unity that is inherent and fundamental to being in Christ. This unity occurs by the grace of God when one enters Christ's body. Anyone who has genuinely become a member of the body of Christ has received this unity.

The New Testament world was essentially divided into two communities: Jewish and Gentile. The gulf between these two groups was as wide as any gulf which might exist between any two races today. Yet Paul affirms that Jew and Gentile had become *one* in Christ:

> For He Himself is our peace, who made both groups into one, . . . (Ephesians 2:14).

> . . . that in Himself He might make the two into one new man, thus establishing peace, and might reconcile them both in one body to God through the cross, . . . (Ephesians 2:15, 16).

> There is neither Jew nor Greek, there is neither slave nor free man, there is neither male nor female; for you are all one in Christ Jesus (Galatians 3:28).

Christ, through His death on the cross, has made into one all people who come into Christ, regardless of their backgrounds and race. Jews and Gentiles, two distinct races, are recreated into a new race and are called Christians. Christ does not make Jews into Gentiles or Gentiles into Jews. He does not raise the Gentile up to the position of privilege occupied by the Jew; neither does He bring the Jew down to the position of the Gentile. He raises both Jew and Gentile to a heavenly position in Christ which far transcends any privilege or position ever promised to or possessed by either. The Jew forgets that he is a Jew, and the Gentile forgets that he is a Gentile. Each thinks only of what he is in Christ. Christ is Savior and Lord to both. In this divine oneness, all national, racial, social, and family distinctions are removed.

Through Christ, we are first of all reconciled to God (Colossians 1:20). Second, through that reconciliation, we are reconciled to one another and "are being built together into a dwelling of God in the Spirit" (Ephesians 2:22). Before two can be united with each other, they must first be united with God.

History contains examples of peoples, like the Normans and the Saxons, who were continually at war with each other. Hostility and hatred perpetually characterized them. Through the centuries, however, the peoples intermarried and intertwined, until eventually these two communities of people had merged into one. Thus, the separate nations, as unique communities, ceased to exist. The wars, of course, ended because the division between them no longer existed. The intermingling of the two communities produced one new community of people who loved and respected each other.[2]

In a similar way, all human divisions and barriers are broken down in Christ; one new body of people is created by God's marvelous grace. In His body, we do not see Jew or Greek, slave or freeman, rich man or poor man, male or female, white man or black man. We only see that we "are all one in Christ Jesus" (Galatians 3:28).

In understanding the unity in Christ, then, we must first recognize the organic unity which we receive when we enter His body. It is appropriate, and even necessary, to tell ourselves when we enter the body of Christ that we are now one with all other members of His body. We must think and act in concert with this

---

[2]R. C. Bell, *Studies in Ephesians* (Austin, Tex.: Firm Foundation Publishing House, 1971), 25.

truth. No rank, no barriers, no divisions, and no cliques organically exist in Christ's body. We have become one with Christ and one with each other.

A DOCTRINAL UNITY

Second, we must recognize the doctrinal unity which is found in Christ. An organic unity is given by the Spirit when we enter the body of Christ, but this unity must be maintained by our adherence to the teachings of the Scriptures.

Christians are bound together by a unity of teaching and belief. Christ's body is not a collection of people guided by groundless beliefs about God and dreamy speculations about life. Members of His body are united upon God's divine revelation of truth.

As Paul discussed the unity of the church of Christ, as he urged Christians to preserve the unity of the Spirit in the bond of peace, he named seven "ones" which form the doctrinal foundation for the maintenance of the organic unity in Christ's body. He said, "There is one body and one Spirit, just as also you were called in one hope of your calling; one Lord, one faith, one baptism, one God and Father of all who is over all and through all and in all" (Ephesians 4:4-6). The body of which Paul wrote is the spiritual body of Christ, the church (Ephesians 1:22, 23). The Spirit is the third member of the Godhead who gave us the revelation of the Scriptures. The one hope is the eternal hope which girds the heart of every Christian through the gospel (Colossians 1:23). The one Lord is the Christ, the Son of the living God, the one who died for our sins and was raised for our justification. The one faith is the belief in Christ and His Word which is engendered by the testimony of the Scriptures (Romans 10:17). The one baptism is the baptism which Christ commanded in the Great Commission and which will be in effect until the end of the Christian Age (Matthew 28:19, 20). The one God is the eternal God who is Creator and Sustainer of the earth, the only true and living God. Concerning the seven "ones," R. C. Bell said, "These unalterable, final facts demand either acceptance or repudiation. No other reaction is possible; a man who rejects even one of them is not to consider himself a Christian at all."[3]

God seeks to bring all the clanging discord in His world into a harmonious unity in Christ.

Union is one thing, but unity is another. Union can be achieved by coercion, but unity can only be found in devotion. Union can be created by binding two people together with ropes, but unity can only come when hearts are bound together with faith and love. The pioneer preachers said, "One can take two tomcats, tie their tails together, and throw them across a clothesline, and he would have union, but not unity." People of divided minds and wills can experience a type of union, but people can only dwell together in one accord through speaking the same things and being one in mind and judgment.

Paul not only pleaded for unity in 1 Corinthians 1:10, but he specified the kind of unity for which he pleaded—a unity of agreement, without divisions, complete in mind and judgment. This kind of unity is

---

[3]Ibid., 24.

brought about by a submission to Christ's will. In Acts 2, on the day the church was established, each person submitted to the message of the Spirit delivered by inspired men. This submission resulted in doctrinal unity: "And they were continually devoting themselves to the apostles' teaching. . . . And all those who had believed were together, and had all things in common" (Acts 2:42-44). Understandably, then, Paul wrote to the brethren in Philippi, "Let us keep living by that same standard to which we have attained" (Philippians 3:16).

A PRACTICAL UNITY

Third, a practical unity must characterize the body of Christ. The organic unity which is given by the Holy Spirit when we enter Christ must be maintained by not only each member's adherence to the plain teachings of the Scriptures but also by each member's adopting a practical, common-sense approach to living together in one accord in Christ.

Paul admonished the Philippian brethren to manifest the attitude of "live-togetherism." He said, "Make my joy complete by being of the same mind, maintaining the same love, united in spirit, intent on one purpose" (Philippians 2:2). He further said, "I urge Euodia and I urge Syntyche to live in harmony in the Lord" (Philippians 4:2). These verses necessarily demand that each member of Christ's body live by the teachings of the Bible and keep his opinions, and sometimes even his wishes, to himself.

We are never to put a brother in a position where, if he does what we demand, he would violate his conscience. Paul said,

Therefore let us not judge one another anymore, but rather determine this—not to put an obstacle or a stumbling block in a brother's way (Romans 14:13).

Now we who are strong ought to bear the weaknesses of those without strength and not just please ourselves. Let each of us please his neighbor for his good, to his edification. For even Christ did not please Himself; but as it is written, "The reproaches of those who reproached Thee fell upon Me" (Romans 15:1-3).

Ben Franklin once said that if a man is trying to get two boards to fit together perfectly, it may be necessary for him to saw off both of the ends that are to fit. In other words, practical unity often requires give-and-take. The selfish man will never know unity with others. He will always live in a little kingdom which is bounded on all four sides by his selfish demands. He cannot come out of that kingdom for genuine fellowship with others, and no one else can enter it for genuine fellowship with him.

This practical unity in Christ grows out of a conscious attempt on the part of each member of Christ's body to consider his brother or sister with love and grace. He is to devalue his opinions and even his wishes. He is to do nothing from selfishness or empty conceit, but with humility of mind, he is to regard others as more important than himself (Philippians 2:3). He is not to look out for his own interests; he is to look out for the interests of others (Philippians 2:4). As he so lives, he is uniquely exhibiting the mind of Christ (Philippians 2:5-8).

CONCLUSION

Christ's body, therefore, is to be characterized by unity. This unity has a threefold character: an organic nature, a doctrinal nature, and a practical nature. The organic unity comes by God's grace upon our entrance into His body. It is maintained and experienced through a doctrinal and practical unity resulting from a conscious commitment to the teachings of the Scriptures and to the spiritual life of other Christians.

God seeks to bring all the clanging discord in His world into a harmonious unity in Christ: "For it was the Father's good pleasure for all the fulness to dwell in Him, and through Him to reconcile all things to Himself, having made peace through the blood of His cross; through Him, I say, whether things on earth or things in heaven" (Colossians 1:19, 20). Christ, through His gospel, calls us to this unity in His body. God planned it (Ephesians 3:6), Christ prayed for it and provided the possibility for it (John 17:21; Ephesians 2:16), Paul pleaded for it (1 Corinthians 1:10), and the Spirit produces it (Ephesians 4:1-6).

Should we not accept this unity by receiving it and abiding in it?

QUESTIONS FOR STUDY
AND DISCUSSION

1. In what way is unity in Christ both pleasant and good?
2. What was Christ's special prayer for His church the night before His crucifixion? (See John 17:21-24.)
3. Discuss the admonition for unity given by Paul in 1 Corinthians 1:10.

4. Define the organic unity which Christ's church has.
5. When is the organic unity of the church given to one who is entering the church?
6. Define the doctrinal unity of the church. What is the difference between the organic and doctrinal unity of the church?
7. Discuss R. C. Bell's statement about the seven "ones."
8. What is the difference between unity and union?
9. How are unity and submission to the will of Christ related?
10. Define the practical unity that we are to have in Christ.
11. What is the difference between the doctrinal unity and the practical unity of the church?
12. What are some common-sense steps one can take in maintaining the practical unity of the church?

14

Which Is the New Testament Church?

"So we, who are many, are one body in Christ, and individually members one of another" (Romans 12:5).

Of necessity, accountable living in this world requires making decisions. We might even say that life, when boiled down to the basics, consists of two traits: time in this world and decision-making.

Most of our decisions are small, momentary, and somewhat insignificant. They affect our living briefly and then are forgotten. Other decisions are influential and determinative. They cast long shadows and affect our living not only today but also our futures. They will either help us or haunt us tomorrow. Consequently, a poorly-made major decision is often regretted for a lifetime.

We make some of our decisions hurriedly and without much thought, with our response being given so quickly that it is like a reaction. These decisions do not weigh heavily on our minds before or after the decisions are made. Other decisions require deep thought and a careful weighing of the evidence which may stretch into weeks or months.

Some decisions are so critically important that they affect the way we will live before God in this life and will determine our eternal destiny. These decisions which influence life and eternity require serious thinking and prayerful research before being made.

These truths about decision-making remind us that no more far-reaching decision perhaps could be considered than the decision proposed by the question "Which is the New Testament church?" The decision we make regarding this question will influence our daily living for God, our spiritual identity, our worship, and our spiritual service. This question, then, must be thoughtfully considered until it is answered according to the clear teachings of the Scriptures and our best unprejudiced reasoning.

Our world is filled with different churches which plead for our commitment and allegiance. A decision must be made. Which is the New Testament church? How shall we decide?

Common-sense guidelines obviously must be followed to help us think carefully about the evidence and make the right choice, the choice which will please God. If we follow these guidelines with integrity, we can identify the New Testament church in the world today.

What are these guidelines?

CONSIDER ITS BEGINNING

One of the identifying marks of the New Testament church is the time of its beginning. Any church which began at a different time from the New Testament church is obviously not the New Testament church.

Three-fourths of the way through His personal ministry, Jesus promised, "I will build My church" (Matthew 16:18). He fulfilled His promise on the first Pentecost Day following His resurrection (Acts 2:41-47). From this Pentecost Day forward, the church is spoken of as being in existence throughout the rest of the New Testament (Acts 5:11; 7:38; 8:1, 3).

No denomination of any kind is found in the New Testament.

Suppose someone said, "My church started in the Old Testament." His church is too early. The Old Testament predicts the coming of the kingdom, but it does not record its establishment. Suppose someone said, "My church started during the third century A.D." His church is too late. This cannot be the New Testament church. The New Testament does not end looking for the establishment of the church some day in the future. Rather, it ends with the Roman Empire quaking under the mighty spread of the church throughout the world.

In general, the Protestant churches sprang into existence during the sixteenth century, during or after the Reformation. No denomination of any kind is found in the New Testament. The New Testament church was established, and then centuries later, as apostasies from the New Testament order began to occur, denominations were formed. The picture in the New Testament is that of people becoming Christians, living, and worshiping as the body of Christ long before any denominations came into existence.

As you consider a specific church, ask, "When was

its actual beginning?" If it goes back to any time other than the time of the first Pentecost after our Lord's resurrection, it cannot be the New Testament church.

CONSIDER ITS AIM

Another identifying characteristic of the New Testament church is its purpose or aim. The New Testament church has no other goal in this world but to be the New Testament church. It does not seek to be similar to it, akin to it, or nearly it. It intends to be it!

When considering the question "Which is the New Testament church?" you can ask of a specific church, "What is its aim or purpose in this world?" The New Testament church was the body of Christ in the world. Paul said, "So we, who are many, are one body in Christ, and individually members one of another" (Romans 12:5). Any church that is not seeking to be the body of Christ in its community is simply not the New Testament church.

The body of Christ in the New Testament could not have been made up of denominations, inasmuch as denominations did not exist in the first century. It was made up of individual Christians who had entered that body by belief in Jesus (Acts 16:31), repentance (Acts 2:38), confession of Jesus as the Son of God and Lord (Romans 10:10), and baptism for the forgiveness of sins (Acts 22:16). As the body of Christ, they met together for worship and fellowship in the communities where they lived (Acts 2:42). Those Christians were not the body of Christ and something else; they were not called by another name as they sought to be the body of Christ; they were just the body of Christ, the church of Christ (Romans 16:16). They worshiped together, looked out after each other, and carried on

God's work together with a unity that is illustrated by the unity that adheres between the members of a physical body.

Christ did not call people to be His disciples by being a denomination. He called them to be His disciples by being His body in the world. This body is to wear His name, worship together in His name, and do His work in the world for His glory.

CONSIDER ITS PRACTICES

Still another identifying mark of the New Testament church is its practices. It is one thing to say that a church is the New Testament church, but it is quite another for that church to demonstrate its identity by its practices. Anyone can claim to be the New Testament church, but the proof of the claim is always in the practice.

The practices of the New Testament church are easily seen in the New Testament. The New Testament church met for worship on the first day of the week and broke bread in remembrance of the Lord's death. This was done every first day of the week (Acts 20:7; 1 Corinthians 11:20; Hebrews 10:25). Christians would sing together, making melody in their hearts and edifying one another. The New Testament contains no record of the use of instrumental music in their worship nor any command for them to do so (Ephesians 5:19; Colossians 3:16). They gave of their material prosperity on the first day of each week for the carrying on of God's work and the helping of the poor (1 Corinthians 16:1, 2). They prayed together and considered God's will which was being revealed by inspired men (Acts 2:42). Each congregation of the New Testament church governed itself through overseers or elders (1 Timothy 3:1-7), looking to Jesus as the only head of the church. Deacons (1 Timothy 3:8-11) and evangelists (2 Timothy 4:1, 2) served the church under the oversight of the elders.

Suppose I had several bicycles in front of my house and I offered to give you one of them if you could find it. You would immediately ask, "What are its characteristics?" so that you could find it. If I said, "It is red in color, has on its handlebars a wire basket containing six apples, and has two red reflectors on its back fender," you would know exactly what to do. You would go outside and look at the bicycles there, and you would attempt to match the characteristics I had named with one of the bicycles in front of my house. When you had made the match, you would claim that bicycle as your own in harmony with the agreement we had made.

Is our task not the same today in identifying the New Testament church? We must list the characteristic practices of the New Testament church and then compare this list with the churches we see around us. When we find a true match, when we find a church which follows the New Testament pattern, we have found the New Testament church, the Lord's church.

CONSIDER ITS DESIGNATIONS

Another identifying mark of the New Testament church is its designations. The descriptive phrases which are used for the New Testament church in the Bible are revealing and distinguishing.

The New Testament church is designated in the New Testament as "the body of Christ" (Ephesians 4:12), "the church of God" (1 Corinthians 1:2), "the churches of Christ" (Romans 16:16), the "church of the first-born" (Hebrews 12:23), "the kingdom of heaven" (Matthew 16:19), and simply "the church" (Ephesians 1:22). These designations describe the nature and identity of the church. They are descriptive phrases more than they are names.

What if you are considering a church which is designated by a phrase or name which is not found in the New Testament? Surely we must admit that this is unacceptable. First, if this church is the New Testament church, why does it use a designation for itself which is foreign to the New Testament? Second, if this church is the New Testament church, why does it not use the New Testament designation for the church to indicate to all that it is the New Testament church?

By God's grace, the honest seeker of truth can identify the New Testament church in the world today.

Third, it is possible for a New Testament church to be using a phrase foreign to the New Testament as a designation without really thinking about it. Surely, when this is called to their attention, they will gladly change to the New Testament designations so that no one will mistake them for something other than the New Testament church.

Designations are important. They identify and distinguish. It is true that a rose by any other name is still a rose, as William Shakespeare said. However, if a lily wanted to become a rose and wanted everyone to know that it had become a rose, it would not only want to take on the characteristics of a rose, but it would want to call itself a rose. If a lily wanted to become a rose, had taken on the characteristics of a rose, and wanted everyone to know that it is a rose, it would not make sense for it to call itself anything other than a rose.

So it is with the church. If a church wants to be the New Testament church, has taken on the characteristics of the New Testament church, and wants everyone to know that it is the New Testament church, it should apply to itself the designations given in the New Testament for the New Testament church and only those.

CONCLUSION

By God's grace, the honest seeker of truth can identify the New Testament church in the world today. Four guidelines which are especially helpful in identifying the Lord's church are these: (1) Look at its beginning, (2) look at its aim, (3) look at its practices, and (4) look at its designations. When these characteristics are used as identifying features, one can readily determine the true church from the false ones.

While walking down a crowded hallway in the building where I teach each day, I heard a student say, "Dr. Cloer, wait just a minute!" I stopped and turned around to see a student rushing up to me to ask a question. I had been walking down a hallway among dozens of students and professors, but I was different from every one of them and was recognized and singled out by this student. How did he pick me out? All of us have characteristics and uniquenesses which make us different from everyone else. Our facial appearances, our body builds, our mannerisms, our voices, and many other traits enter into making up our composite uniqueness. We are different from everyone else, and everyone who knows us sees that difference.

Through its unique characteristics, the New Testament church stands out from all the manmade churches of the world. When we look at its special traits, we are able to distinguish the Lord's church from them. It will require, however, weighing the evidence, making unbiased comparisons, and asking pointed questions.

Should we settle for anything but the New Testament church? Who would want to?

Why be a substitute when we can be the real thing?

QUESTIONS FOR STUDY
AND DISCUSSION

1. Why is deciding which is the New Testament church a far-reaching decision?
2. List verses of Scripture which show that the New Testament church began on the Day of Pentecost in Acts 2.
3. When did denominations spring up?
4. What is the goal of the New Testament church?
5. Who composes the body of Christ—individual Christians or denominational churches? (See 1 Corinthians 12:24.)
6. Did Christ call His disciples to be denominations in this world? How do you know?
7. What are the practices of the New Testament church?
8. Should churches today follow the practices of the New Testament church?
9. How is the New Testament church designated in the New Testament?
10. Why should a church which is seeking to be the New Testament church designate itself the same way the church in the New Testament is designated?

11. Why are designations important?
12. Is it realistic to believe that we should be able to distinguish and identify the New Testament church today?

Appendix 1

The Words "Church" and "Churches" in the New Testament

"In answering any religious question, we must begin with the basic question 'What does the Bible actually say about it?'"

The word "church" appears seventy-nine times in the New Testament, and the word "churches" appears thirty-five times. An examination of the use of these two words in the New Testament reveals that the words are used in six different contexts. For a better understanding of the nature of the New Testament church, study carefully the different contexts in which these words are used.

First, the word "church" is used to mean a secular assembly called together for a special purpose or a secular assembly which just occurs. (See Acts 19:32, 39, 41.) Second, it is used in a universal sense, or in reference to all of God's people, regardless of their geographical location in the world. (See Matthew 16:18.) Third, it is used in a compositional sense, or in reference to the saved of a specific racial background. (See Romans 16:4). Fourth, it is used in a regional sense, or in reference to the churches of a given general area. (See Galatians 1:2 and Acts 9:31.) Fifth, the word is used for the saved in a given locality, as a reference to a specific group of Christians worshiping and working together for Christ's glory in a definite location. (See 1 Corinthians 1:2 and Colossians 4:16.) Sixth, it is used in reference to the assembly of Christians for worship and study. (See 1 Corinthians 11:18.)

Study carefully the use the Holy Spirit made of these two words in the New Testament. Noted beside each phrase title is the number of times the word or expression appears in the New Testament.

"Church" (79)

Matthew (3)

Matthew 16:18
"'And I also say to you that you are Peter, and upon this rock I will build My church; and the gates of Hades shall not overpower it.'"

Matthew 18:17
"'And if he refuses to listen to them, tell it to the church: and if he refuses to listen even to the church, let him be to you as a Gentile and a tax-gatherer.'"

Acts (21)

Acts 2:47
"Praising God, and having favor with all the people. And the Lord was adding to their number day by day those who were being saved."

(The KJV has "church," but manuscript evidence is poor for its appearance in Acts 2:47.)

Acts 5:11
"And great fear came upon the whole church, and upon all who heard of these things."

Acts 7:38
"'This is the one who was in the congregation [*ekklesia*; church] in the wilderness together with the angel who was speaking to him on Mount Sinai, and who was with our fathers; . . .'"

Acts 8:1
". . . And on that day a great persecution arose against the church in Jerusalem; and they were all scattered throughout the regions of Judea and Samaria, except the apostles."

Acts 8:3
"But Saul began ravaging the church, entering house after house; and dragging off men and women, he would put them in prison."

Acts 9:31
"So the church throughout all Judea and Galilee and Samaria enjoyed peace, being built up; and, going on in the fear of the Lord and in the comfort of the Holy Spirit, it continued to increase."

Acts 11:22
"And the news about them reached the ears of the church at Jerusalem, and they sent Barnabas off to Antioch."

Acts 11:26
". . . And it came about that for an entire year they met
with the church, and taught considerable numbers;
and the disciples were first called Christians in Antioch."

Acts 12:1
"Now about that time Herod the king laid hands on
some who belonged to the church, . . ."

Acts 12:5
"So Peter was kept in the prison, but prayer for him
was being made fervently by the church to God."

Acts 13:1
"Now there were at Antioch, in the church that was
there, prophets and teachers: Barnabas, and Simeon
who was called Niger, and Lucius of Cyrene, and
Manaen who had been brought up with Herod the
tetrarch, and Saul."

Acts 14:23
"And when they had appointed elders for them in
every church, having prayed with fasting, they com-
mended them to the Lord in whom they had believed."

Acts 14:27
"And when they had arrived and gathered the church
together, they began to report all things that God had
done with them and how He had opened a door of
faith to the Gentiles."

Acts 15:3
"Therefore, being sent on their way by the church, they

were passing through both Phoenicia and Samaria, describing in detail the conversion of the Gentiles, and were bringing great joy to all the brethren."

Acts 15:4
"And when they arrived at Jerusalem, they were received by the church and the apostles and the elders, and they reported all that God had done with them."

Acts 15:22
"Then it seemed good to the apostles and the elders, with the whole church, to choose men from among them to send to Antioch with Paul and Barnabas. . . ."

Acts 18:22
"And when he had landed at Caesarea, he went up and greeted the church, and went down to Antioch."

Acts 19:32
"So then, some were shouting one thing and some another, for the assembly [ekklesia; church] was in confusion, . . ."

Acts 19:39
"'But if you want anything beyond this, it shall be settled in the lawful assembly [ekklesia; church].'"

Acts 19:40, 41
"'For indeed we are in danger of being accused of a riot in connection with today's affair, since there is no real cause for it; and in this connection we shall be unable to account for this disorderly gathering.' And after saying this he dismissed the assembly [ekklesia; church]."

Acts 20:17
"And from Miletus he sent to Ephesus and called to
him the elders of the church."

Acts 20:28
"'Be on guard for yourselves and for all the flock,
among which the Holy Spirit has made you overseers,
to shepherd the church of God which He purchased
with His own blood.'"

Romans (3)

Romans 16:1
"I commend to you our sister Phoebe, who is a servant
of the church which is at Cenchrea."

Romans 16:5
"Also greet the church that is in their house, . . ."

Romans 16:23
"Gaius, host to me and to the whole church, greets you
. . . ."

1 Corinthians (16)

1 Corinthians 1:2
"To the church of God which is at Corinth, to those
who have been sanctified in Christ Jesus, saints by
calling, with all who in every place call upon the name
of our Lord Jesus Christ, their Lord and ours."

1 Corinthians 4:17
"For this reason I have sent to you Timothy, who is my
beloved and faithful child in the Lord, and he will
remind you of my ways which are in Christ, just as I

teach everywhere in every church."

1 Corinthians 6:4
"If then you have law courts dealing with matters of this life, do you appoint them as judges who are of no account in the church?"

1 Corinthians 10:32
"Give no offense either to Jews or to Greeks or to the church of God."

1 Corinthians 11:18
"For, in the first place, when you come together as a church, I hear that divisions exist among you; and in part, I believe it."

1 Corinthians 11:22
"What! Do you not have houses in which to eat and drink? Or do you despise the church of God, and shame those who have nothing? . . ."

1 Corinthians 12:28
"And God has appointed in the church, first apostles, second prophets, third teachers, then miracles, then gifts of healings, helps, administrations, various kinds of tongues."

1 Corinthians 14:4
"One who speaks in a tongue edifies himself; but one who prophesies edifies the church."

1 Corinthians 14:5
"Now I wish that you all spoke in tongues, but even more that you would prophesy; and greater is one who

prophesies than one who speaks in tongues, unless
he interprets, so that the church may receive edifying."

1 Corinthians 14:12
"So also you, since you are zealous of spiritual gifts,
seek to abound for the edification of the church."

1 Corinthians 14:19
"However, in the church I desire to speak five words
with my mind, that I may instruct others also, rather
than ten thousand words in a tongue."

1 Corinthians 14:23
"If therefore the whole church should assemble together and all speak in tongues, and ungifted men or
unbelievers enter, will they not say that you are mad?"

1 Corinthians 14:28
"But if there is no interpreter, let him keep silent in the
church; and let him speak to himself and to God."

1 Corinthians 14:35
"And if they desire to learn anything, let them ask
their own husbands at home; for it is improper for a
woman to speak in church."

1 Corinthians 15:9
"For I am the least of the apostles, who am not fit to be
called an apostle, because I persecuted the church of
God."

1 Corinthians 16:19
"The churches of Asia greet you. Aquila and Prisca

greet you heartily in the Lord, with the church that is in their house."

2 Corinthians (1)

2 Corinthians 1:1
"Paul, an apostle of Christ Jesus by the will of God, and Timothy our brother, to the church of God which is at Corinth. . . ."

Galatians (1)

Galatians 1:13
"For you have heard of my former manner of life in Judaism, how I used to persecute the church of God beyond measure, and tried to destroy it."

Ephesians (9)

Ephesians 1:22
"And He put all things in subjection under His feet, and gave Him as head over all things to the church."

Ephesians 3:10
"In order that the manifold wisdom of God might now be made known through the church to the rulers and the authorities in the heavenly places."

Ephesians 3:21
"To Him be the glory in the church and in Christ Jesus to all generations forever and ever. Amen."

Ephesians 5:23
"For the husband is the head of the wife, as Christ also is the head of the church, He Himself being the Savior of the body."

Ephesians 5:24
"But as the church is subject to Christ, so also the wives ought to be to their husbands in everything."

Ephesians 5:25
"Husbands, love your wives, just as Christ also loved the church and gave Himself up for her."

Ephesians 5:27
"That He might present to Himself the church in all her glory, . . ."

Ephesians 5:29
"For no one ever hated his own flesh, but nourishes and cherishes it, just as Christ also does the church."

Ephesians 5:32
"This mystery is great; but I am speaking with reference to Christ and the church."

Philippians (2)

Philippians 3:6
"As to zeal, a persecutor of the church; . . ."

Philippians 4:15
"And you yourselves also know, Philippians, that at the first preaching of the gospel, after I departed from Macedonia, no church shared with me in the matter of giving and receiving but you alone."

Colossians (4)

Colossians 1:18
"He is also head of the body, the church; and He is the

beginning, the first-born from the dead; so that He Himself might come to have first place in everything."

Colossians 1:24
"Now I rejoice in my sufferings for your sake, and in my flesh I do my share on behalf of His body (which is the church) in filling up that which is lacking in Christ's afflictions."

Colossians 4:15
"Greet the brethren who are in Laodicea and also Nympha and the church that is in her house."

Colossians 4:16
"And when this letter is read among you, have it also read in the church of the Laodiceans; and you, for your part read my letter that is coming from Laodicea."

1 Thessalonians (1)

1 Thessalonians 1:1
"Paul and Silvanus and Timothy to the church of the Thessalonians in God the Father and the Lord Jesus Christ: Grace to you and peace."

2 Thessalonians (1)

2 Thessalonians 1:1
"Paul and Silvanus and Timothy to the church of the Thessalonians in God our Father and the Lord Jesus Christ."

1 Timothy (3)

1 Timothy 3:5
"(But if a man does not know how to manage his own

household, how will he take care of the church of
God?)"

1 Timothy 3:15
"But in case I am delayed, I write so that you may
know how one ought to conduct himself in the household of God, which is the church of the living God, the
pillar and support of the truth."

1 Timothy 5:16
"If any woman who is a believer has dependent wid-
ows, let her assist them, and let not the church be
burdened, . . ."

Philemon (1)

Philemon 2
". . . and to the church in your house."

Hebrews (2)

Hebrews 2:12
"Saying, 'I will proclaim Thy name to My brethren, in
the midst of the congregation [*ekklesia*; church] I will
sing Thy praise.'"

Hebrews 12:23
"To the general assembly and church of the first-born
who are enrolled in heaven, and to God, the Judge of
all, and to the spirits of righteous men made perfect."

James (1)

James 5:14
"Is anyone among you sick? Let him call for the elders

of the church, and let them pray over him, anointing him with oil in the name of the Lord."

3 John (3)

3 John 6
"And they bear witness to your love before the church; and you will do well to send them on their way in a manner worthy of God."

3 John 9
"I wrote something to the church; but Diotrephes, who loves to be first among them, does not accept what we say."

3 John 10
". . . and he forbids those who desire to do so, and puts them out of the church."

Revelation (7)

Revelation 2:1
"'To the angel of the church in Ephesus write: The One who holds the seven stars in His right hand, the One who walks among the seven golden lampstands, says this.'"

Revelation 2:8
"'And to the angel of the church in Smyrna write: The first and the last, who was dead, and has come to life, says this.'"

Revelation 2:12
"'And to the angel of the church in Pergamum write: The One who has the sharp two-edged sword says this.'"

Revelation 2:18
"'And to the angel of the church in Thyatira write: The Son of God, who has eyes like a flame of fire, and His feet are like burnished bronze, says this.'"

Revelation 3:1
"And to the angel of the church in Sardis write: He who has the seven Spirits of God, and the seven stars, says this: 'I know your deeds, that you have a name that you are alive, but you are dead.'"

Revelation 3:7
"'And to the angel of the church in Philadelphia write: He who is holy, who is true, who has the key of David, who opens and no one will shut, and who shuts and no one opens, says this.'"

Revelation 3:14
"'And to the angel of the church in Laodicea write: The Amen, the faithful and true Witness, the Beginning of the creation of God, says this.'"

"Churches" (35)

Acts (2)

Acts 15:41
"And he was traveling through Syria and Cilicia, strengthening the churches."

Acts 16:5
"So the churches were being strengthened in the faith, and were increasing in number daily."

Romans (2)

Romans 16:4
"Who for my life risked their own necks, to whom not only do I give thanks, but also all the churches of the Gentiles."

Romans 16:16
"Greet one another with a holy kiss. All the churches of Christ greet you."

1 Corinthians (6)

1 Corinthians 7:17
"Only, as the Lord has assigned to each one, as God has called each, in this manner let him walk. And thus I direct in all the churches."

1 Corinthians 11:16
"But if one is inclined to be contentious, we have no other practice, nor have the churches of God."

1 Corinthians 14:33
"For God is not a God of confusion but of peace, as in all the churches of the saints."

1 Corinthians 14:34
"Let the women keep silent in the churches; for they are not permitted to speak, but let them subject themselves, just as the Law also says."

1 Corinthians 16:1
"Now concerning the collection for the saints, as I directed the churches of Galatia, so do you also."

1 Corinthians 16:19
"The churches of Asia greet you. Aquila and Prisca greet you heartily in the Lord, with the church that is in their house."

2 Corinthians (8)

2 Corinthians 8:1
"Now, brethren, we wish to make known to you the grace of God which has been given in the churches of Macedonia."

2 Corinthians 8:18
"And we have sent along with him the brother whose fame in the things of the gospel has spread through all the churches."

2 Corinthians 8:19
"And not only this, but he has also been appointed by the churches to travel with us in this gracious work, which is being administered by us for the glory of the Lord Himself, and to show our readiness."

2 Corinthians 8:23
"As for Titus, he is my partner and fellow worker among you; as for our brethren, they are messengers of the churches, a glory to Christ."

2 Corinthians 8:24
"Therefore openly before the churches show them the proof of your love. . . ."

2 Corinthians 11:8
"I robbed other churches, taking wages from them to serve you."

2 Corinthians 11:28
"Apart from such external things, there is the daily pressure upon me of concern for all the churches."

2 Corinthians 12:13
"For in what respect were you treated as inferior to the rest of the churches, except that I myself did not become a burden to you? Forgive me this wrong!"

Galatians (2)

Galatians 1:2
"And all the brethren who are with me, to the churches of Galatia."

Galatians 1:22
"And I was still unknown by sight to the churches of Judea which were in Christ."

1 Thessalonians (1)

1 Thessalonians 2:14
"For you, brethren, became imitators of the churches of God in Christ Jesus that are in Judea, for you also endured the same sufferings at the hands of your own countrymen, even as they did from the Jews."

2 Thessalonians (1)

2 Thessalonians 1:4
"Therefore, we ourselves speak proudly of you among the churches of God for your perseverance and faith in the midst of all your persecutions and afflictions which you endure."

Revelation (13)

Revelation 1:4
"John to the seven churches that are in Asia: Grace to you and peace, from Him who is and who was and who is to come; and from the seven Spirits who are before His throne."

Revelation 1:11
"Saying, 'Write in a book what you see, and send it to the seven churches: to Ephesus and Smyrna and to Pergamum and to Thyatira and to Sardis and to Philadelphia and to Laodicea.'"

Revelation 1:20
"'As for the mystery of the seven stars which you saw in My right hand, and the seven golden lampstands: the seven stars are the angels of the seven churches, and the seven lampstands are the seven churches.'"

Revelation 2:7, 11, 17, 29; 3:6, 13, 22
"'He who has an ear, let him hear what the Spirit says to the churches. . . .'"

Revelation 2:23
"'And I will kill her children with pestilence; and all the churches will know that I am He who searches the minds and hearts; and I will give to each one of you according to your deeds.'"

Revelation 22:16
"'I, Jesus, have sent My angel to testify to you these things for the churches. I am the root and the offspring of David, the bright morning star.'"

Appendix 2

The Words "Kingdom" and "Kingdoms" in the New Testament

"If we do not allow the Scriptures to truly be our divine authority by searching them carefully and following them in detail, we have no authority save our own manmade traditions and our own inaccurate human wisdom."

The basic meaning of the word "kingdom" in the New Testament is "rule, power, or sovereignty." The kingdom of God, therefore, is the rule or sovereignty of God.

The word "kingdom" appears in about six different contexts in the New Testament. The word "kingdom" appears 157 times in the New Testament, and the word "kingdoms" is found three times. First, the word "kingdom" is used in reference to a secular, earthly, political rule. For example, it is used this way in the plural in Matthew 4:8. Second, it is used in reference to the kingdom of Israel. God was the king of Israel, and Israel was His kingdom. (See Matthew 8:12.) Third, it is used simply in reference to the power or rule of God. When someone bows to the will of God, he has, in a preparatory sense, entered the kingdom of God. (See Matthew 12:28.) Fourth, it is used in reference to the church, the special rule of God on earth today. (See Matthew 11:11; 16:18; John 3:5; Colossians 1:13.) Fifth, it is used in reference to heaven as the eternal kingdom of God. (See Luke 13:28.) Sixth, it is used of Satan's realm of dominion. (See Matthew 12:26.)

Matthew predominantly uses the phrase "kingdom of heaven." Mark, Luke, and John use, without exception, the phrase "kingdom of God." The two phrases obviously have the same meaning.

Study carefully the use the Holy Spirit made of the word "kingdom" in the New Testament. Noted beside each phrase title is the number of times that particular word or expression appears in the New Testament.

"A kingdom" (2)

Luke (1)

Luke 22:29, 30
"'And just as My Father has granted Me a kingdom, I grant you that you may eat and drink at My table in My kingdom, . . .'"

Hebrews (1)

Hebrews 12:28
"Therefore, since we receive a kingdom which cannot be shaken, let us show gratitude, by which we may offer to God an acceptable service with reverence and awe."

"The kingdom" (11)

Matthew (4)

Matthew 6:13
"'And do not lead us into temptation, but deliver us from evil. [For Thine is the kingdom, and the power, and the glory, forever. Amen.]'"
(The last sentence of this verse is not found in most reliable manuscripts.)

Matthew 8:12
"But the sons of the kingdom shall be cast out into the outer darkness; in that place there shall be weeping and gnashing of teeth."

Matthew 13:19
"'When anyone hears the word of the kingdom, and does not understand it, the evil one comes and snatches away what has been sown in his heart. This is the one on whom seed was sown beside the road.'"

Matthew 13:38
"'And the field is the world; and as for the good seed, these are the sons of the kingdom; and the tares are the sons of the evil one.'"

Matthew 25:34
"'Then the King will say to those on His right, "Come, you who are blessed of My Father, inherit the kingdom prepared for you from the foundation of the world."'"

Mark (1)

Mark 11:10
"Blessed is the coming kingdom of our father David;

Hosanna in the highest!"

Luke (1)

Luke 12:32
"'Do not be afraid, little flock, for your Father has chosen gladly to give you the kingdom.'"

Acts (2)

Acts 1:6
"And so when they had come together, they were asking Him, saying, 'Lord, is it at this time You are restoring the kingdom to Israel?'"

Acts 20:25
"'And now, behold, I know that all of you, among whom I went about preaching the kingdom, will see my face no more.'"

1 Corinthians (1)

1 Corinthians 15:24
"Then comes the end, when He delivers up the kingdom to the God and Father, when He has abolished all rule and all authority and power."

James (1)

James 2:5
"Listen, my beloved brethren: did not God choose the poor of this world to be rich in faith and heirs of the kingdom which He promised to those who love Him?"

Revelation (1)

Revelation 1:9
"I, John, your brother and fellow partaker in the

tribulation and kingdom and perseverance which are in Jesus, . . ."

"Kingdom of heaven" (31)

Matthew (31)

Matthew 3:2
"'Repent, for the kingdom of heaven is at hand.'"

Matthew 4:17
"From that time Jesus began to preach and say, 'Repent, for the kingdom of heaven is at hand.'"

Matthew 5:3
"'Blessed are the poor in spirit, for theirs is the kingdom of heaven.'"

Matthew 5:10
"'Blessed are those who have been persecuted for the sake of righteousness, for theirs is the kingdom of heaven.'"

Matthew 5:19
"'Whoever then annuls one of the least of these commandments, and so teaches others, shall be called least in the kingdom of heaven; but whoever keeps and teaches them, he shall be called great in the kingdom of heaven.'"

Matthew 5:20
"'For I say to you, that unless your righteousness surpasses that of the scribes and Pharisees, you shall not enter the kingdom of heaven.'"

Matthew 7:21
"'Not everyone who says to Me, "Lord, Lord," will enter the kingdom of heaven; but he who does the will of My Father who is in heaven.'"

Matthew 8:11
"'And I say to you, that many shall come from east and west, and recline at the table with Abraham, and Isaac, and Jacob, in the kingdom of heaven.'"

Matthew 11:11
"'Truly, I say to you, among those born of women there has not arisen anyone greater than John the Baptist; yet he who is least in the kingdom of heaven is greater than he.'"

Matthew 11:12
"'And from the days of John the Baptist until now the kingdom of heaven suffers violence, and violent men take it by force.'"

Matthew 13:11
"And He answered and said to them, 'To you it has been granted to know the mysteries of the kingdom of heaven, but to them it has not been granted.'"

Matthew 13:24
"He presented another parable to them, saying, 'The kingdom of heaven may be compared to a man who sowed good seed in his field.'"

Matthew 13:31
"He presented another parable to them, saying, 'The kingdom of heaven is like a mustard seed, which a

man took and sowed in his field.'"

Matthew 13:33
"He spoke another parable to them, 'The kingdom of
heaven is like leaven, which a woman took, and hid in
three pecks of meal, until it was all leavened.'"

Matthew 13:44
"'The kingdom of heaven is like a treasure hidden in
the field, which a man found and hid; and from joy
over it he goes and sells all that he has, and buys that
field.'"

Matthew 13:45
"'Again, the kingdom of heaven is like a merchant
seeking fine pearls.'"

Matthew 13:47
"'Again, the kingdom of heaven is like a dragnet cast
into the sea, and gathering fish of every kind.'"

Matthew 13:52
"And He said to them, 'Therefore every scribe who
has become a disciple of the kingdom of heaven is like
a head of a household, who brings forth out of his
treasure things new and old.'"

Matthew 16:19
"'I will give you the keys of the kingdom of heaven;
and whatever you shall bind on earth shall be bound
in heaven, and whatever you shall loose on earth shall
be loosed in heaven.'"

Matthew 18:1
"At that time the disciples came to Jesus, saying, 'Who

then is greatest in the kingdom of heaven?'"

Matthew 18:3
"And said, 'Truly I say to you, unless you are converted and become like children, you shall not enter the kingdom of heaven.'"

Matthew 18:4
"'Whoever then humbles himself as this child, he is the greatest in the kingdom of heaven.'"

Matthew 18:23
"'For this reason the kingdom of heaven may be compared to a certain king who wished to settle accounts with his slaves.'"

Matthew 19:12
"For there are eunuchs who were born that way from their mother's womb; and there are eunuchs who were made eunuchs by men; and there are also eunuchs who made themselves eunuchs for the sake of the kingdom of heaven. He who is able to accept this, let him accept it."

Matthew 19:14
"But Jesus said, 'Let the children alone, and do not hinder them from coming to Me; for the kingdom of heaven belongs to such as these."

Matthew 19:23
"And Jesus said to His disciples, 'Truly, I say to you, it is hard for a rich man to enter the kingdom of heaven.'"

Matthew 20:1
"'For the kingdom of heaven is like a landowner who

went out early in the morning to hire laborers for his vineyard.'"

Matthew 22:2
"'The kingdom of heaven may be compared to a king, who gave a wedding feast for his son.'"

Matthew 23:13
"'But woe to you, scribes and Pharisees, hypocrites, because you shut off the kingdom of heaven from men; for you do not enter in yourselves, nor do you allow those who are entering to go in.'"

Matthew 25:1
"'Then the kingdom of heaven will be comparable to ten virgins, who took their lamps, and went out to meet the bridegroom.'"

"The gospel of the kingdom" (3)

Matthew (3)

Matthew 4:23
"And Jesus was going about in all Galilee, teaching in their synagogues, and proclaiming the gospel of the kingdom, and healing every kind of disease and every kind of sickness among the people."

Matthew 9:35
"And Jesus was going about all the cities and the villages, teaching in their synagogues, and proclaiming the gospel of the kingdom, and healing every kind of disease and every kind of sickness."

Matthew 24:14
"'And this gospel of the kingdom shall be preached in

the whole world for a witness to all the nations, and then the end shall come.'"

"Kingdom of God" (67)

Matthew (4)

Matthew 12:28
"'But if I cast out demons by the Spirit of God, then the kingdom of God has come upon you.'"

Matthew 19:24
"'And again I say to you, it is easier for a camel to go through the eye of a needle, than for a rich man to enter the kingdom of God.'"

Matthew 21:31
"'Which of the two did the will of his father?' They said, 'The latter.' Jesus said to them, 'Truly I say to you that the tax-gatherers and harlots will get into the kingdom of God before you.'"

Matthew 21:43
"'Therefore I say to you, the kingdom of God will be taken away from you, and be given to a nation producing the fruit of it.'"

Mark (14)

Mark 1:15
"And saying, 'The time is fulfilled, and the kingdom of God is at hand; repent and believe in the gospel.'"

Mark 4:11
"And He was saying to them, 'To you has been given

the mystery of the kingdom of God; but those who are outside get everything in parables.'"

Mark 4:26
"And He was saying, 'The kingdom of God is like a man who casts seed upon the soil.'"

Mark 4:30
"And He said, 'How shall we picture the kingdom of God, or by what parable shall we present it?'"

Mark 9:1
"And He was saying to them, 'Truly I say to you, there are some of those who are standing here who shall not taste death until they see the kingdom of God after it has come with power.'"

Mark 9:47
"'And if your eye causes you to stumble, cast it out; it is better for you to enter the kingdom of God with one eye, than having two eyes, to be cast into hell.'"

Mark 10:14
"But when Jesus saw this, He was indignant and said to them, 'Permit the children to come to Me; do not hinder them; for the kingdom of God belongs to such as these.'"

Mark 10:15
"'Truly I say to you, whoever does not receive the kingdom of God like a child shall not enter it at all.'"

Mark 10:23
"And Jesus, looking around, said to His disciples,

'How hard it will be for those who are wealthy to enter the kingdom of God!'"

Mark 10:24
"And the disciples were amazed at His words. But Jesus answered again and said to them, 'Children, how hard it is to enter the kingdom of God!'"

Mark 10:25
"'It is easier for a camel to go through the eye of a needle than for a rich man to enter the kingdom of God.'"

Mark 12:34
"And when Jesus saw that he had answered intelligently, He said to him, 'You are not far from the kingdom of God. . . .'"

Mark 14:25
"'Truly I say to you, I shall never again drink of the fruit of the vine until that day when I drink it new in the kingdom of God.'"

Mark 15:43
"Joseph of Arimathea came, a prominent member of the Council, who himself was waiting for the kingdom of God; and he gathered up courage and went in before Pilate, and asked for the body of Jesus."

Luke (32)

Luke 4:43
"But He said to them, 'I must preach the kingdom of God to the other cities also, for I was sent for this purpose.'"

Luke 6:20
"And turning His gaze on His disciples, He began to say, 'Blessed are you who are poor, for yours is the kingdom of God.'"

Luke 7:28
"'I say to you, among those born of women, there is no one greater than John; yet he who is least in the kingdom of God is greater than he.'"

Luke 8:1
"And it came about soon afterwards, that He began going about from one city and village to another, proclaiming and preaching the kingdom of God; and the twelve were with Him."

Luke 8:10
"And He said, 'To you it has been granted to know the mysteries of the kingdom of God, but to the rest it is in parables, ...'"

Luke 9:2
"And He sent them out to proclaim the kingdom of God, and to perform healing."

Luke 9:11
"But the multitudes were aware of this and followed Him; and welcoming them, He began speaking to them about the kingdom of God and curing those who had need of healing."

Luke 9:27
"'But I say to you truthfully, there are some of those

standing here who shall not taste death until they see the kingdom of God.'"

Luke 9:60
"But He said to him, 'Allow the dead to bury their own dead; but as for you, go and proclaim everywhere the kingdom of God.'"

Luke 9:62
"But Jesus said to him, 'No one, after putting his hand to the plow and looking back, is fit for the kingdom of God.'"

Luke 10:9
"'And heal those in it who are sick, and say to them, "The kingdom of God has come near to you."'"

Luke 10:11
"'"Even the dust of your city which clings to our feet, we wipe off in protest against you; yet be sure of this, that the kingdom of God has come near."'"

Luke 11:20
"'But if I cast out demons by the finger of God, then the kingdom of God has come upon you.'"

Luke 13:18
"Therefore He was saying, 'What is the kingdom of God like, and to what shall I compare it?'"

Luke 13:20
"And again He said, 'To what shall I compare the kingdom of God?'"

Luke 13:28
"'There will be weeping and gnashing of teeth there when you see Abraham and Isaac and Jacob and all the prophets in the kingdom of God, but yourselves being cast out.'"

Luke 13:29
"'And they will come from east and west, and from north and south, and will recline at the table in the kingdom of God.'"

Luke 14:15
"And when one of those who were reclining at the table with Him heard this, he said to Him, 'Blessed is everyone who shall eat bread in the kingdom of God!'"

Luke 16:16
"'The Law and the Prophets were proclaimed until John; since then the gospel of the kingdom of God is preached, and everyone is forcing his way into it.'"

Luke 17:20
"Now having been questioned by the Pharisees as to when the kingdom of God was coming, He answered them and said, 'The kingdom of God is not coming with signs to be observed.'"

Luke 17:21
"'Nor will they say, "Look, here it is!" or "There it is!" For behold, the kingdom of God is in your midst.'"

Luke 18:16
"But Jesus called for them, saying, 'Permit the children to come to Me, and do not hinder them, for the king-

dom of God belongs to such as these.'"

Luke 18:17
"'Truly I say to you, whoever does not receive the kingdom of God like a child shall not enter it at all.'"

Luke 18:24
"And Jesus looked at him and said, 'How hard it is for those who are wealthy to enter the kingdom of God!'"

Luke 18:25
"'For it is easier for a camel to go through the eye of a needle, than for a rich man to enter the kingdom of God.'"

Luke 18:29, 30
"And He said to them, 'Truly I say to you, there is no one who has left house or wife or brothers or parents or children, for the sake of the kingdom of God, who shall not receive many times as much at this time and in the age to come, . . .'"

Luke 19:11
"And while they were listening to these things, He went on to tell a parable, because He was near Jerusalem, and they supposed that the kingdom of God was going to appear immediately."

Luke 21:31
"'Even so you, too, when you see these things happening, recognize that the kingdom of God is near.'"

Luke 22:16
"'For I say to you, I shall never again eat it until it is

fulfilled in the kingdom of God.'"

Luke 22:18
"'For I say to you, I will not drink of the fruit of the vine from now on until the kingdom of God comes.'"

Luke 23:50, 51
"And behold, a man named Joseph, . . . (he had not consented to their plan and action), a man from Arimathea, a city of the Jews, who was waiting for the kingdom of God."

John (2)

John 3:3
"Jesus answered and said to him, 'Truly, truly, I say to you, unless one is born again, he cannot see the kingdom of God.'"

John 3:5
"Jesus answered, 'Truly, truly, I say to you, unless one is born of water and the Spirit, he cannot enter into the kingdom of God.'"

Acts (6)

Acts 1:3
"To these He also presented Himself alive, after His suffering, by many convincing proofs, appearing to them over a period of forty days, and speaking of the things concerning the kingdom of God."

Acts 8:12
"But when they believed Philip preaching the good news about the kingdom of God and the name of Jesus

Christ, they were being baptized, men and women alike."

Acts 14:22
"Strengthening the souls of the disciples, encouraging them to continue in the faith, and saying, 'Through many tribulations we must enter the kingdom of God.'"

Acts 19:8
"And he entered the synagogue and continued speaking out boldly for three months, reasoning and persuading them about the kingdom of God."

Acts 28:23
"And when they had set a day for him, they came to him at his lodging in large numbers; and he was explaining to them by solemnly testifying about the kingdom of God, and trying to persuade them concerning Jesus, from both the Law of Moses and from the Prophets, from morning until evening."

Acts 28:31
"Preaching the kingdom of God, and teaching concerning the Lord Jesus Christ with all openness, unhindered."

Romans (1)

Romans 14:17
"For the kingdom of God is not eating and drinking, but righteousness and peace and joy in the Holy Spirit."

1 Corinthians (4)

1 Corinthians 4:20
"For the kingdom of God does not consist in words,

but in power."

1 Corinthians 6:9
"Or do you not know that the unrighteous shall not inherit the kingdom of God? . . ."

1 Corinthians 6:10
"Nor thieves, nor the covetous, nor drunkards, nor revilers, nor swindlers, shall inherit the kingdom of God."

1 Corinthians 15:50
"Now I say this, brethren, that flesh and blood cannot inherit the kingdom of God; nor does the perishable inherit the imperishable."

Galatians (1)

Galatians 5:21
"Envying, drunkenness, carousing, and things like these, of which I forewarn you just as I have forewarned you that those who practice such things shall not inherit the kingdom of God."

Colossians (1)

Colossians 4:11
"And also Jesus who is called Justus; these are the only fellow workers for the kingdom of God who are from the circumcision; and they have proved to be an encouragement to me."

2 Thessalonians (1)

2 Thessalonians 1:5
"This is a plain indication of God's righteous judgment

so that you may be considered worthy of the kingdom of God, for which indeed you are suffering."

Revelation (1)

Revelation 12:10
"And I heard a loud voice in heaven, saying, "Now the salvation, and the power, and the kingdom of our God and the authority of His Christ have come, . . ."

Kingdom of Christ (15):
"The eternal kingdom of our Lord and Savior Jesus Christ," "The kingdom of our Lord," "His kingdom," "His heavenly kingdom," "The kingdom of His beloved Son," "My kingdom," "Your kingdom"

Matthew (3)

Matthew 13:41
"'The Son of Man will send forth His angels, and they will gather out of His kingdom all stumbling blocks, and those who commit lawlessness.'"

Matthew 16:28
"'Truly I say to you, there are some of those who are standing here who shall not taste death until they see the Son of Man coming in His kingdom.'"

Matthew 20:21
"And He said to her, 'What do you wish?' She said to Him, 'Command that in Your kingdom these two sons of mine may sit, one on Your right and one on Your left.'"

Luke (3)

Luke 1:33
"And He will reign over the house of Jacob forever; and His kingdom will have no end."

Luke 22:30
"'That you may eat and drink at My table in My kingdom, . . .'"

Luke 23:42
"And he was saying, 'Jesus, remember me when You come in Your kingdom!'"

John (3)

John 18:36
"Jesus answered, 'My kingdom is not of this world. If My kingdom were of this world, then My servants would be fighting, that I might not be delivered up to the Jews; but as it is, My kingdom is not of this realm.'"

Colossians (1)

Colossians 1:13
"For He delivered us from the domain of darkness, and transferred us to the kingdom of His beloved Son."

2 Timothy (2)

2 Timothy 4:1
"I solemnly charge you in the presence of God and of Christ Jesus, who is to judge the living and the dead, and by His appearing and His kingdom."

2 Timothy 4:18
"The Lord will deliver me from every evil deed, and

will bring me safely to His heavenly kingdom; to Him be the glory forever and ever. Amen."

Hebrews (1)

Hebrews 1:8
"But of the Son He says, 'Thy throne, O God, is forever and ever, and the righteous scepter is the scepter of His kingdom.'"

2 Peter (1)

2 Peter 1:11
"For in this way the entrance into the eternal kingdom of our Lord and Savior Jesus Christ will be abundantly supplied to you."

Revelation (1)

Revelation 11:15
"And the seventh angel sounded; and there arose loud voices in heaven, saying, 'The kingdom of the world has become the kingdom of our Lord, and of His Christ; and He will reign forever and ever.'"

The Father's kingdom (7):
"Thy kingdom,"
"The kingdom of their Father,"
"My Father's kingdom,"
"His own kingdom"
"His kingdom," "Our kingdom"

Matthew (4)

Matthew 6:10
"'Thy kingdom come. Thy will be done, on earth as it is in heaven.'"

Matthew 6:33
"'But seek first His kingdom and His righteousness;
and all these things shall be added to you.'"

Matthew 13:43
"'Then the righteous will shine forth as the sun in the
kingdom of their Father. . . .'"

Matthew 26:29
"'But I say to you, I will not drink of this fruit of the
vine from now on until that day when I drink it new
with you in My Father's kingdom.'"

Luke (2)

Luke 11:2
"And He said to them, 'When you pray, say: "Father,
hallowed be Thy name. Thy kingdom come."'"

Luke 12:31
"But seek for His kingdom, and these things shall be
added to you."

1 Thessalonians (1)

1 Thessalonians 2:12
"So that you may walk in a manner worthy of the God
who calls you into His own kingdom and glory."

"The kingdom of Christ and God" (1)

Ephesians (1)

Ephesians 5:5
"For this you know with certainty, that no immoral or
impure person or covetous man, who is an idolater,

has an inheritance in the kingdom of Christ and God."

Earthly "kingdom" or "kingdoms" (20)
"Kingdoms of the world,"
"Their kingdom," "My [Herod's] kingdom"

Matthew (4)

Matthew 4:8
"Again, the devil took Him to a very high mountain, and showed Him all the kingdoms of the world, and their glory."

Matthew 12:25
"And knowing their thoughts He said to them, 'Any kingdom divided against itself is laid waste; and any city or house divided against itself shall not stand.'"

Matthew 24:7
"For nation will rise against nation, and kingdom against kingdom, and in various places there will be famines and earthquakes."

Mark (5)

Mark 3:24
"And if a kingdom is divided against itself, that kingdom cannot stand."

Mark 6:23
"And he [Herod] swore to her, 'Whatever you ask of me, I will give it to you; up to half of my kingdom.'"

Mark 13:8
"For nation will rise against nation, and kingdom against kingdom; there will be earthquakes in various

places; there will also be famines. These things are merely the beginning of birth pangs."

Luke (6)

Luke 4:5
"And he led Him up and showed Him all the kingdoms of the world in a moment of time."

Luke 11:17
"But He knew their thoughts, and said to them, 'Any kingdom divided against itself is laid waste; and a house divided against itself falls.'"

Luke 19:12
"He said therefore, 'A certain nobleman went to a distant country to receive a kingdom for himself, and then return.'"

Luke 19:15
"And it came about that when he returned, after receiving the kingdom, he ordered that these slaves, to whom he had given the money, be called to him in order that he might know what business they had done.'"

Luke 21:10
"Then He continued by saying to them, 'Nation will rise against nation, and kingdom against kingdom.'"

Hebrews (1)

Hebrews 11:33
"Who by faith conquered kingdoms, performed acts of righteousness, obtained promises, shut the mouths of lions."

Revelation (4)

Revelation 11:15
"And the seventh angel sounded; and there arose loud voices in heaven, saying, 'The kingdom of the world has become the kingdom of our Lord, and of His Christ; and He will reign forever and ever.'"

Revelation 17:12
"And the ten horns which you saw are ten kings, who have not yet received a kingdom, but they receive authority as kings with the beast for one hour."

Revelation 17:17
"For God has put it in their hearts to execute His purpose by having a common purpose, and by giving their kingdom to the beast, until the words of God should be fulfilled."

Revelation 17:18
"And the woman whom you saw is the great city, which reigns over the kings of the earth."
(The Greek text has "a kingdom over the kings of the earth.")

Satan's Kingdom (3)
"His kingdom"

Matthew (1)

Matthew 12:26
"'And if Satan casts out Satan, he is divided against himself; how then shall his kingdom stand?'"

Luke (1)

Luke 11:18
"'And if Satan also is divided against himself, how shall his kingdom stand/ For you say that I cast out demons by Beelzebul.'"

Revelation (1)

Revelation 16:10
"And the fifth angel poured out his bowl upon the throne of the beast; and his kingdom became darkened; and they gnawed their tongues because of pain.'"

Bibliography

Bales, J. D. *The Cross and the Church*. Shreveport, La.: Lambert Book House, 1974.

Bell, R. C. *Studies in Ephesians*. Austin, Tex.: Firm Foundation Publishing Company, 1971.

Bright, John. *The Kingdom of God*. Nashville, Tenn.: Abingdon, 1953.

Campbell, Alexander. *The Christian System*. St. Louis, Mo.: Christian Board of Publication, 1839; reprint, Cincinnati, Ohio: Standard Publishing Company, n.d.

Cogdill, Roy E. *The New Testament Church*. Lufkin, Tex.: R. E. Cogdill Publishing Company, 1946.

Elkins, Garland and Thomas B. Warren, eds. *The Church: The Beautiful Bride of Christ*. Jonesboro, Ark.: National Christian Press, 1980.

Ferguson, Everett. *The New Testament Church*. The Way of Life Series. Abilene, Tex.: Biblical Research Press, 1968.

Flew, R. N. *Jesus and His Church*. London: Epworth, 1943.

Genner, E. E. *The Church in the New Testament*. London: Charles H. Kelly, 1914.

Graves, W. C. *Lessons on the Church of Christ*. Birmingham, Al.: W. C. Graves, n.d.

Ladd, George Eldon. *Crucial Questions About the Kingdom of God*. Grand Rapids, Mich.: Wm. B. Eerdmans Publishing Company, 1952.

Larimore, T. B. "Unity." In *Biographies and Sermons*, edited by F. D. Srygley, n.p., n.d.; reprint, Nashville, Tenn.: Gospel Advocate, 1961.

Milligan, Robert. *The Scheme of Redemption*. n.p., 1868; reprint, St. Louis, Mo.: The Bethany Press, 1962.

Minear, Paul. *Images of the Church in the New Testament*. Philadelphia: Westminster Press, 1960.

Paxson, Ruth. *The Wealth, Walk, and Warfare of the Christian*. Old Tappan, N.J.: Fleming H. Revell Company, 1939.

Phillips, Thomas W. *The Church of Christ*. Cincinnati, Ohio: Standard Publishing Company, 1943.

Schweizer, Eduard. *The Church as the Body of Christ*. Richmond, Va.: John Knox, 1964.

Stott, John R. W. *What Christ Thinks of the Church*. Grand Rapids, Mich.: Wm. B. Eerdmans Publishing Company, 1958.

Thomas, J. D., ed. *God's Eternal Purpose*, Abilene Christian College Bible Lectures. Abilene, Tex.: Abilene Christian College Book Store, 1969.

Wilson, L. R. *The New Testament Church: A Divine Institution*. Austin, Tex.: Firm Foundation Publishing Company, 1953.

A Free Bible Study

Would you like to study more about the church in the New Testament? You can enroll in a World Bible School Correspondence Course, free of charge.

For further study of the Bible, send your name and complete mailing address to the address below. You will be contacted by a teacher who will study with you through a Bible Correspondence Course as you explore the Word of God and gain a better understanding of the New Testament.

World Bible School Correspondence Course
2209 S. Benton
Searcy, AR 72143